WATCHING COSMIC TIME

WATCHING COSMIC TIME

The Suspense Films of Hitchcock, Welles, and Reed

MATTHEW DWIGHT MOORE

CASCADE *Books* • Eugene, Oregon

WATCHING COSMIC TIME
The Suspense Films of Hitchcock, Welles, and Reed

Copyright © 2022 Matthew Dwight Moore. All rights reserved. Except for brief quotations in critical publications or reviews, no part of this book may be reproduced in any manner without prior written permission from the publisher. Write: Permissions, Wipf and Stock Publishers, 199 W. 8th Ave., Suite 3, Eugene, OR 97401.

Cascade Books
An Imprint of Wipf and Stock Publishers
199 W. 8th Ave., Suite 3
Eugene, OR 97401

www.wipfandstock.com

PAPERBACK ISBN: 978-1-6667-3262-7
HARDCOVER ISBN: 978-1-6667-2653-4
EBOOK ISBN: 978-1-6667-2654-1

Cataloguing-in-Publication data:

Names: Moore, Matthew Dwight, author.

Title: Watching cosmic time : the suspense films of Hitchcock, Welles, and Reed / by Matthew Dwight Moore.

Description: Eugene, OR: Cascade Books, 2022 | | Includes bibliographical references and index.

Identifiers: ISBN 978-1-6667-3262-7 (paperback) | ISBN 978-1-6667-2653-4 (hardcover) | ISBN 978-1-6667-2654-1 (ebook)

Subjects: LCSH: Space and time in motion pictures. | Hitchcock, Alfred, 1899–1980—Criticism and interpretation. | Welles, Orson, 1915–1985—Criticism and interpretation. | Reed, Carol, 1906–1976—Criticism and interpretation. | Thrillers (Motion pictures)—History and criticism.

Classification: PN1995.9.D4 M667 2022 (paperback) | PN1995.9.D4 (ebook)

10/24/22

To Sara, my beloved

Contents

Acknowledgments	ix
Chapter One: Double Vision: Midcentury Suspense Films	1
Some Examples	5
High Noon (1952)	9
The Big Clock (1948)	13
Chapter Two: *Shadow of a Doubt* (1943)	18
Salvific Order	18
The Moral Imperative	26
Community Clockwork	31
Citizens on Patrol	36
Missing the Train	40
Uncle Charlie, Antichrist	45
Chapter Three: *The Stranger* (1946)	49
For Him the Bell Tolls	50
Stranger in a Strange Land	55
Establish Time	61
Frontier Justice	65
Holy Family	73
Killing Time	78
Chapter Four: *Odd Man Out* (1947)	84
Another Way Ahead	85
Odd Man In	91
Disorderly Conduct	97
Microcosmic Time and Space	102
Christology/Chronology	107
The Ultimate Authorities	111
Conclusion: Things to Come	114
Bibliography	119
Index	125

Acknowledgments

For their contributions to this book, my thanks go out to the following. Stan Rubin, Greta Niu, Monika Mehta, Joseph Keith, and Leslie Heywood all provided constructive criticism at the earliest stages of this work's development. I owe my father and mother, Carl and Bonnie Moore, so much that it is foolish to try to articulate. My daughter Lydia and son Malcolm graciously lent me out to this project for long swaths of time. My colleagues at Roberts Wesleyan College, whom I have been honored to call friends, C. Harold Hurley, Jud Decker, David Basinger, Andy Koehl, Michael Landrum, Linda Quinlan, Romy Hosford, and J. Richard Middleton, helped me in so many indirect ways. The assistance of Stan Pelkey, Elizabeth Whittingham, Matthew Ballard, Meredith Ader, and Sara Wolcott is warmly appreciated. I am thankful for the assistance of Sophia Lorent of the George Eastman Museum. I am also thankful for Karen (Ren) van Meenen of *Afterimage* and Rochester Institute of Technology for so many things. This project would be unthinkable without one of the best free public library systems in the country, my own Monroe County Public Library System and all their skilled librarians. This book would not exist without Binghamton University, the George Eastman Museum, or SUNY College at Brockport. Thanks also to the British Film Institute, ITV, and NBC Universal. My great gratitude goes out to Elijah Davidson, as well as those at Cascade Books—Chris Spinks, Matthew Wimer, George Callihan, Kara Barlow, Brian Palmer, Savanah N. Landerholm, and Stephanie Hough—who clearly have been supportive of this work.

Most importantly, I am thankful beyond words for my best friend and wife of many years, Sara Zavacki-Moore, who has remained supportive and loving during our multiple shared and suspenseful adventures in life.

CHAPTER ONE

Double Vision: Midcentury Suspense Films

By the beginning of cinema in the mid-1890s, the world's time zones had been standardized—a measure of how mechanistic the West's fetishization of time had become. This standardization process illustrates how highly polyvalent it was. Multiple issues arose concerning the interaction of church and state. There were technological obstacles in synchronizing old, ornate church clocks with others. The standardization of time zones, developed by train corporations by the 1880s, in effect compelled governments to comply in the interest of community order. As Peter Galison writes, "Time reformation had passed from a myriad of competing simultaneities to a tightly coordinated fact, plucked from telescopes, confirmed by humming iron rails, then wired into metropolitan clocks."[1]

In mechanistic time societies, such as the ones now common throughout the modern technocratic world, when a person comes late to church or a court appearance, for example, they will likely be read as being morally lax, irresponsible, unlawful, or even sinful. Crudely put, late is bad. And this negative correlation was perpetuated by the modern polyvalent institutions of church and state. Film emerged in this context.

The advent of cinema in the late Victorian period helped reify the commonly held belief that the universe is intrinsically orderly, a belief one could term *the cosmological presumption*. What cinema provided that was novel was the opportunity to construct the cosmological presumption as a suspenseful, time-based microcosm. Cinema produced new formats to

1. Galison, *Einstein's Clocks*, 128.

watch time, reflect upon the ways time is constructed, and even speak to such received notions about time. In this regard, cinema could be considered to have helped sustain a politico-religious memeplex, of which the cosmological presumption is but a facet. Instead of conceptualizing modern religion as being subsumed by the state, Michel Foucault dismisses this secularization hypothesis in favor of polyvalence, asserting that "modern states begin to take shape while Christian structures tighten their grip on individual existence."[2] If that is so, it may be a valuable project to explore the ways in which the cinema apparatus has hosted such a memeplex through the paradox of revealing and obscuring.

The cinematic cosmological presumption requires a kind of *scotomaphilia*, or "love of blind spots." On the one hand, normally, viewers mentally, socially, and even morally construct a rationale or logic for a watched film in order to make sense of it. But this construction of order is also built on a valuation of what is not seen. The persistence of vision experienced while watching a film is constructed in the absence of moving images—or any images at all. As images flicker before the viewer's eye at, say, twenty-four frames per second (a cinematic standard), the images rarely entirely overlap. Instead, during the very brief intervals *in between* successive images, the eye looks at a blank screen. In this way, the viewer takes an active part in the creation and meaning of the film, if only on a cognitive level. Film audiences have become socialized to participate in this scotomaphilia. Mark Jancovich explains this in these terms:

> Narrative concerns the loss of a sense of wholeness (the disruption of order); the search for that which is lacking (the process of disorder); and finally the recovery of that which is lost (narrative resolution). However, it should be pointed out that ... the sense of lack can never be filled, so narrative is ultimately unable to achieve complete resolution. The text provides substitutes for the missing object, but can never finally portray the moment of wholeness and completion.[3]

Audiences may feel excited, provoked, or satisfied by their film-watching experiences, but, as Jancovich says, never entirely satisfied because cinema ultimately represents an intrinsic absence. Absence is presence. Contemporary studies in cognitive psychology and neuroscience seem to show how all perceptual systems operate by this form of biased mental construction—a construction that produces concomitant suspense out of this tension.

2. Foucault, *Abnormal*, 177.
3. Jancovich, "Screen Theory," 140.

All cinema is suspenseful. Even avant-garde or nonnarrative films are suspenseful. The act of watching a film is based on the anticipation of narrative resolution from disorder back to order. Order is the default status of cinema. It preexists the watching of a film, although it can never offer a complete or synoptic experience of order. This is true of any of the visual evidence used in seeing time as order. As temporally and spatially limited beings, we simply cannot watch everything or fully apprehend cosmic time. We must necessarily make conceptual leaps in order to apprehend the fundamental nature of the universe. The creation of meaning seems founded on transforming absence into presence and chaos into continuity. Since films are also necessarily limited, watching a film is also an exercise in suspense. As Mary Ann Doane observes:

> Suspense is predicated on absence or separation and driven by an external threat to the home, the family, the woman. The gap between shots mimics the gap constitutive of desire. Suspense in the cinema . . . is on the side of invisibility, and depends upon the activation of off-screen space, or the "blind-spot."[4]

The cinematic cosmological presumption which is predicated on scotomaphilia also mimics the gap constitutive of desire.

A film that features a clock, for example, acts on a variety of interrelated phenomena. The viewer psychologically projects a presumption of order on the film that is being physically projected. As long as continuity editing predominates, the experience is not only seen as orderly, but time-based as well. Watching a clock in a motion picture doubles this time-as-order experience. It is metachronic in the sense that the *clock* simultaneously shows the passage of time while the *film* shows the passage of time. Both, presumably, must be orderly.

During the midcentury period the coalescence of global and cinematic suspense produced a handful of films that seem to employ clocks as connotative emblems. These films made it possible both to watch cosmic time and reflect on the modes of constructing the cosmological presumption. They explicitly and self-reflexively appropriate the historical emblems of time as order (e.g., clocks) to situate the belief in an orderly universe as a focus for cinematic interrogation.

The specific geohistorical context of these films was the *chaoskampf*, or global apocalyptic conflict through war. Although this notion is an ancient one, the latest modern technocratic version emerged in Europe just before WWI (contemporaneous with the development of film). This *chaoskampf*

---

4. Doane, *Emergence of Cinematic Time*, 195.

did not see a kind of climax until the end of the "total war" experience in the 1940s, when worldwide populations were first able to acknowledge the vastness of the *hemoclysm*, or bloodbath, that eclipsed the lives of approximately one hundred million human beings. In a way, a profound scotomaphilia was writ large when film images showing the devastation at Hiroshima and Nagasaki were largely suppressed by the United States government in August 1945. Audiences were allowed access to some newsreels of Nazi genocide but were unable to view film footage of the atomic attacks by their own forces on Japanese civilians for twenty-five years—squarely into the era of the Vietnam War.

The first real agents of the cinematic cosmological presumption were born at the turn of the century. This generation grew up in a world that had already begun producing widespread feature-length films. The cinematic mode of watching cosmic time was already naturalized for them during their maturation into modern technocracy. For example, as Christian Metz notes, cinema had become a "doubly temporal sequence . . . [that invited audiences] to consider that one of the functions of narrative is to invent one time scheme in terms of another time scheme."[5]

Members of this first generation of the cinematic cosmological presumption such as Adolf Hitler, Dwight Eisenhower, Charlie Chaplin, Albert Einstein, and Alfred Hitchcock reached adulthood approximately by WWI. By the midcentury period these leaders were at least middle aged and had survived the experience of the Great War. They had become the politicians, generals, directors, scientists, and producers. They also carried with them the imprint of the cosmos-chaos discontinuity experienced in the Great War. So this worldview that projected the fantasy of cosmic order dramatically contrasted with the conflation of ostensibly chaotic world events (e.g., war, devastation, and economic collapse) during the developmental stages of this generation's maturation. The war experience marked the (literally) violent discontinuity between the cosmological presumption and the real horrors of geopolitical chaos. The films produced in this era resided in the interplay between these discontinuities. Some of the most extreme cinematic exponents of this were produced by the avant-garde, Dadaists, and surrealists, who used cinema to question the very nature of time, consciousness, and the cosmological presumption. Notwithstanding, mainstream films such as Alfred Hitchcock's *Shadow of a Doubt* (1943), Orson Welles's *The Stranger* (1946), and Carol Reed's *Odd Man Out* (1947) beautifully illustrate the metachronic nature of these midcentury suspense films.

---

5. Metz, *Film Language*, 18.

Not all suspenseful midcentury films demonstrate the double vision effect. David Lean's *The Bridge on the River Kwai* (1957) is indeed a suspenseful midcentury film that is situated culturally and historically in loose relation with the sensibilities of many other films' personnel and worldviews. Although it exploits the cinematic techniques of suspense quite effectively and even replicates the associative effect of mechanistic time in the conclusion as the train progressively sounds its gradual proximity to destruction, *The Bridge on the River Kwai* does not do so self-reflexively or by using specific visual references to the emblems of timekeeping. It therefore does not represent the double vision, or metachronic effect, as fully as some other films.

A few other films of the midcentury period come close to fully exploiting the double vision so manifest in *Shadow of a Doubt*, *The Stranger*, and *Odd Man Out*. This double vision is acutely noticeable in some portions of Walt Disney's animated features *Cinderella* (1950), *Alice in Wonderland* (1951), and *Peter Pan* (1953), as well as Donen and Kelly's musical *On the Town* (1949), Vincente Minnelli's romantic drama *The Clock* (1945), Fred Zinneman's Western *High Noon* (1952), and John Farrow's suspense film *The Big Clock* (1948). All demonstrate different permutations of this book's central concerns but in less obsessive ways. Still, the value of articulating how these relate to the rest of the films that will be analyzed in subsequent chapters should be noted.

SOME EXAMPLES

Walt Disney's animated features *Cinderella* (1950), *Alice in Wonderland* (1951), and *Peter Pan* (1953) use the clock as an emblem of cosmic order. In *Cinderella*, the clock mediates Cinderella's transformation from a subject to the potential head of state by marriage. According to the prescription of the fairy godmother, Cinderella's false identity (fabricated by magical means) will dissolve at 12:00 midnight. Cinderella predictably reverts to her former self promptly at 12:00 outside the prince's ball. This transformation is therefore an expression of a cosmic order that is intrinsically linked with time and the mechanistic emblem of that time. Set against the backdrop of royal decorum and concomitant geopolitical statecraft, the clock marks the liminal state between fantasy and reality.

In *Alice in Wonderland* the film, like Lewis Carroll's book on which it is based, Alice's entrance into Wonderland is mediated by a watch. As Alice dozes in a liminal state at the outset, a white rabbit dashes by her, grasping a pocket watch and declaring "I'm late. I'm late." The declaration of untimeliness becomes the rabbit's mantra and leads Alice to follow him as he disappears into a magical world of topsy-turvydom. The trope of lateness as transgression seems to fill the rabbit with the dread that is often associated with mechanistic time. Being on time is a responsibility embedded in the education of young people in the West. To be late is to transgress the inexplicable rules that undergird the phantasmagoric adult world of schedules and clocks. Alice's world is literally turned upside down as she enters into a perversion of the modern world's conventions and symbols. She eventually reemerges into modern life, and order is sustained after her absurd oneiric journey.

Similarly, Disney's *Peter Pan* uses the clock to mediate the passage from the modern, mechanistic world to the fantastic one that transcends traditional logic, reason, and knowledge. As Peter leads the Darling children on their first flight with fairy dust, they visit the iconic clock tower at the Houses of Parliament. They fly up to the clockface and gently rest on the clock's enormous hand, which moves as they sit on it. The movement is synchronized with the tolling of Big Ben. They then commence their magical flight to Neverland, which is in the direction of "the second star to the right and straight on till morning." This kind of directional specificity simulates both the style of premodern dead reckoning navigation and astronomical coordination. Wendy is also in a liminal state, this time poised between childhood and adulthood. The clock marks the transition between the modern, mechanistic, rational West and the magical, whimsical fantasy of Neverland. Hence, the most famous clock in the world signifies the passage from modernity to a fantastic version of premodernity, where Enlightenment pirates in seventeenth-century costume, premodern Indians, and fairy-tale mermaids interrelate in juxtaposition with each other. Big Ben's presence also evokes the time imperium that characterizes Victorian use of chronometry. The threat that mechanistic time poses invades Neverland in the form of the Crocodile that has swallowed a clock. In essence, the animal and the machine have become one synthesis. The persistent ticking of Tick-Tock the crocodile haunts Captain Hook and serves as a constant reminder of his imminent mortality, even as childhood in general seems immortal.

The conventions of children's animated films had already been established by the midcentury period and were identified by children's special access into fantastical times and places. The films' young audiences were most likely to identify with the surreal obstacles faced by the characters, echoing their own experiences with the double-challenge of maturation and modernity. Here, the suspense of temporality, or suspense emerging from the double vision effect, is key since childhood itself is normally treated merely as a transitional phase into adulthood that will be transformed into a mechanistic monad reflecting the mores of the culture into which they were enculturated. Cosmic time is orderly, not necessarily for young audiences (for whom so much must already seem inherently chaotic and malleable) but for young audiences who are enculturated to become agents of mechanistic modern culture. The films, which employ the emblems of mechanistic time, serve as the signposts both of maturity and modernity. As maturation is an inevitable stage in human development, these Disney films suggest, so too is modernity.

The musical *On the Town* (1949), by Stanley Donen and Gene Kelly, is structured around a twenty-four-hour shore leave in New York City. The film, like the stage version, extracts a good deal of humor from the fact that the three protagonists are overwhelmed by the prospect of experiencing all that New York City has to offer "in just one day." The song "A Day in New York" exposes the absurdity of such an endeavor, but the desire to experience the essence of a city is nonetheless poignant for men who have been confined by the military's strictures for a long duration. The psychoanalytical implication of sublimated libido in the heterosexual, homosocial confines of a deep-sea vessel is that, once liberated in a generally permissive cosmopolitan city, the result will be to express a high degree of repressed energy. Thus, the twenty-four hours become an artificial restriction militating the personal fulfillment of the government's servicemen. The digital clock that scrolls across the screen while the men attempt to see the sights serves as a constant reminder of the prominent role of mechanistic time to the civilian metropolis—as well as the modern military. At various points throughout the film a digital timestamp scrolls across the bottom of the screen, simulating that of the Times Square marquee. This suggests the mock-newsworthiness of the transpiring fictional events.

The initial result of these temporarily liberated servicemen is anarchic. There is disorientation, referenced in the opening song "I Feel Like I'm Not Out of Bed Yet," which captures the paradoxical early morning drowsiness of "the city that never sleeps." The disorientation partially created by the artificially contrived time conditions is also illustrated in "New York, New York," a song that jumbles together the tourist attractions of uptown and downtown—an effect that simulates the conflicted presumed itineraries of harried visitors. The fact that these sailors are linked to an ongoing geopolitical crisis which is at once violent and ubiquitous undercuts the buoyant effect of the film's colorful photography and costumes, quick-tempoed feel-good songs, and predictable happy ending. The location shooting employed in some contemporary films like *The House on 92nd Street* (1945) and *The Naked City* (1948) similarly undercuts the frothy fantasy with a semblance of realism. The male leads of *On the Town* represent government-sanctioned violence. Their sublimation, which could erupt into libidinous anarchy, is ultimately restrained by both the authorities and a lifetime of enculturation into the modes of propriety. At the end of their duration of freedom, they return to their responsibilities at 6:00 a.m. as three more sailors set out to experience the same highs and lows that the three leads just had. The predictability of this satiric and ironic ending reasserts the fundamental (and cyclical) orderliness produced by the temporal institution of the state.

Like *On the Town*, Vincente Minnelli's *The Clock* (1945) operates as a simulation of real time under the contrived conditions of a shore leave, this time lasting forty-eight hours. The protagonist, Corporal Joe Allen, disoriented in New York City, looks for someone to help show him around. He finds that, though pleasant, the strangers he meets are too busy to help him forge an interpersonal connection. These responsible people are propelled by the conventions of mechanistic time, namely, duty and propriety. These conventions are especially cogent in a global *entrepôt* like New York City, where transportation of every kind presumably runs on the accuracy of synchronization and schedule. Joe meets Alice seemingly at random, when she breaks the heel of her shoe over his feet while rushing through Penn Station. The chaotic beginning to their relationship is illustrated first by this accident and next by the drifting camera angle that tries to frame Joe both in foreground and background as he negotiates both directions of the stairs and escalators—not to mention all the busy people—in his attempt to retrieve her broken heel.

The contrivance of a forty-eight-hour leave from military service provides an opportunity for the film to act as microcosmic time. The couple meets, has misadventures, gets separated, gets married, and presumably consummates the marriage, all before he has to leave the final morning. Joe pleads with a store clerk to open his store to fix Alice's shoe, showing the tension created by business time. As with Charlie's lateness in *Shadow of a Doubt*, coming late to an institution was often read by contemporaries as a transgression. As if to emphasize this fact, Joe helps an injured milkman deliver his goods on time in the early hours of the night. The milkman simply cannot be late in delivering milk to his customers. The titular clock at New York's Astor Hotel serves as the rendezvous point for their first date. The clock therefore acts as a specific location in space as well as a machine used to measure time. After a chaotic misadventure through bureaucratic red tape (whose suspense is heightened by the time restrictions of regular office hours) they are perfunctorily married by a justice of the peace in a decidedly secular "service." Alice feels that the civic rite was "ugly" and urges Joe to go with her into a nearby church in order to experience a greater connection to a religious institution, which he agrees to do. The tacit endorsement of both institutions set against the marriage sacrament highlights the cosmic themes. The fact that Joe is an experienced serviceman, much like the three sailors in *On the Town*, connects him with the geopolitical struggle that was transitioning into an era of new global anxieties in 1945. They are literally employed by the state and deployed as needed to quell conflicts around the globe.

HIGH NOON (1952)

Fred Zinneman's iconic Western *High Noon* (1952) also positions watching time in relation to the polyvalence of cosmic order. The film is filled with clocks. At the outset, Will, the town's retiring marshal, is in the process of getting married by the justice of the peace. Amy, his wife, a practicing Quaker, has rehabilitated him from a gun-toting enforcer of the law to a peaceful storekeeper. But immediately after the wedding, Will and Amy (and soon all the residents in town) learn that Frank Miller, his nemesis, was just released from prison and is on his way to kill Will. The clock shows that their wedding ends around 10:35 and Frank's train is set to arrive at "high noon." Consequently, Will periodically checks the time. In this case, watching the clock represents the double vision that characterizes the other films analyzed in this work. Plot and narrative durations nearly synthesize, producing a real-time metachronic effect. In other words, "reel time" is real time. So watching the clock conflates with watching screen time, which itself represents the cosmological presumption. But watching the clock also highlights the heightened significance of these emblems of cosmic order. Situated in relation to the polyvalence of the two main ideological apparatuses (i.e., church and state), the act of watching the clock within the narrative exemplifies the double vision.

Will's acknowledgment of the clock seems to result in certain increasingly intense behaviors. Seeing how much time is left before 12:00 helps him quantify first how much time he has to recruit deputies and (as it becomes apparent that there will be none) how much life he seems to have left to live. Watching time thus produces the cinematic suspense of the film while projecting that suspense onto issues that transcend and supersede his life. Among these issues are the efficacy of law enforcement, the nature of pacifism, the responsibility of citizenry, and the ethical maintenance of order in the world. For example, with an hour to go, Will dutifully attempts to recruit the citizens to take a stand for law and order. By two minutes until noon, he writes his "Last Will and Testament." Will's problem is that there is too little time left. The timekeeping mechanisms link the quest for order to something that transcends the mundane suspense of individual human life.

The first diegetic sound of the film is the chiming of the bell in the church tower on Sunday morning. The first clock appears framed behind Will and Amy as they are married, thus linking their union with the regulation of mechanistic time and the transcendence of cosmic time. Amy later states that she has "one hour" to find out if she will be a wife or a widow. Interestingly, their wedding is conducted in the courthouse, not a church, a point raised by the minister when Will disturbs the Sunday morning service to ask for volunteers to be deputized. They are married in a house of secular law by a representative of civic order. The judge later packs away his scales of justice while recommending that Will leave town, an ultimately unhelpful gesture. The scales of justice, another emblem of cosmic order, thereby reinforce the state's association with the transcendent. The agent of that transcendence turns out to offer little assistance to the temporal (and temporary) enforcer of law and order. Since Will has officially retired, he exists in a legal and moral liminal state—a state of human agency predicated not on representing law and order, but on individual responsibility. He is under no professional or contractual obligation to defend the town. And the brief duration he has to contemplate and act on his role in this cosmic struggle intensifies the suspense of his fate.

The representatives of the official religious institution in town also offer little assistance. Will interrupts the Sunday morning worship service where the minister is preaching from the book of Malachi. The minister admonishes Will for not attending church when he asks for help defending the town. It takes a layman to appeal to the congregation to immediately debate the issue of recruitment within the church building. The use of the sermon Scripture from Malachi 4 is curious here. Traditionally, this last chapter of the book attributed to Malachi marks the final words of the Old Testament before the caesura introducing the Gospel accounts that proclaim the incarnation of Jesus Christ. The presumed historical duration between the writing of Malachi and the writing of the First Gospel is typically believed to be approximately four hundred years—an especially suspenseful duration for those who may have anticipated the fulfillment of the Old Testament's prophecies concerning the coming of Christ. Thus, the reference evokes the expectation of cosmic justice over time. The Malachi passage used by the minister commands Israel to remember the Mosaic law or else God will destroy the land, a threat that resonates with Will's lonely quest. Will's devotion to upholding the principles of law and order, even on threat of humiliation and death, simultaneously responds to Malachi's command and prefigures Jesus as an avatar of cosmic justice and peace.

The democratic debate in the church shows the panoply of responses to Will's position. Some support him outright and agree to be deputized.

Others feel that he should either leave town or avoid violence altogether. The entire debate is infused with reminders of cosmic time. Some argue about "wasting time" by debating, and the mayor urges that they "keep it orderly." The scene is framed by separate scenes that prominently display clocks, the first one near Will's potential deputy Sam Fuller and the other near Will's mentor, Martin Howe. The debating congregation, though democratic, struggles to avoid chaos and is propelled by the suspense represented by the clock. The disorderly tendencies of the congregation are seemingly channeled and controlled by the mayor, acting as de facto facilitator, who ultimately issues a final endorsement of Will's service in which he recommends that Will leave for his own protection.

The polyvalence at work in associating institutions with cosmic order can be discerned in the blurring of lines between church and state. In effect, the courthouse is sacralized and the church is secularized. The courthouse is primarily identified by the act of marriage, which according to the theological and ecclesiastical traditions of Judeo-Christian history has been a prime religious sacrament. Treated with religious reverence, the judge ceremonially folds the flag into his case, as a priest might treat the crucifix or the eucharistic elements. The augmented authority to hold dominion over all aspects of its polity that the state retains is essentially quasi-religious. The judge, like a priest after a religious ceremony, solemnly dismantles the sacred emblems while advising Will about his course of action. On the other hand, the church is secularized by a number of civic interferences. The Sunday morning church service is interrupted by the marshal, an agent of the state who attempts to recruit deputies for a civic matter. Although the minister initially resists, he soon tacitly permits the congregation to use the church's sacred time to entertain a debate. The mayor extemporaneously orchestrates the political discourse which noticeably contrasts with the worshipful setting. The courthouse's sacralization and the church's secularization are connected to the cosmic through the many references to timekeeping that have already been established earlier in the film.

Due to its narrative and its utilization of time fetishism, the film is almost entirely structured on the suspense of temporality. The anticipation of the violent confrontation is itself the subject of the film. The presence of suspense is manifested by the absence of the threat. The identical shots of empty train tracks vanishing into a single-point perspective recur throughout the film. These virtually still shots are devoid of the train's visual and aural presence, and yet they convey through repetition a fetishistic effect that anticipates the train's arrival time. It is implied that this compositional space will soon be filled by Frank Miller's deadly vengeance. Such is the essence of cinematic suspense. But the use of a train (which is by definition literally run on mechanistic time) and the station master's clock seen in the beginning of the film (which reminds us of the global synchronization that marked the transformation from local time to standard time across the West during the late nineteenth century) imbue this suspense with a global and cosmic dimension.

Curiously, Amy's Quakerism is typically invoked only in reference to nonviolence, a traditional stance taken by some Quakers in nearly every Western conflict in the past 350 years. Instead of condemning the use of violence, Quakers have typically avoided making any such doctrinal stance, leaving the matter entirely to the individual conscience, notwithstanding the schism the Society of Friends had been experiencing on the eve of the Civil War.[6] Four years after *High Noon*, Gary Cooper would also star in the film *The Friendly Persuasion* (1956), which dramatized the role of frontier Quakers who conscientiously objected to war. In that film, Cooper similarly plays a man torn by his sense of preserving order in his community on the one hand, and his sense of preserving the sacredness of all life on the other. In both *The Friendly Persuasion* and *High Noon*, Quakers struggle with their own consciences in order to preserve cosmic order. The fact that, at the conclusion of *High Noon*, Amy kills one of Frank Miller's henchmen (by secretly shooting him in the back, no less) is highly poignant specifically because she is a practicing Quaker. It is easy to read her act as tragic (because she betrays her moral code) or cowardly and selfish (since by killing one man she helps save the man she loves). Her blatant act of violence can also be read as one that parallels the individualism manifested in her husband's struggle. Performing justice is typically seen as radiating from the authority of polyvalent institutions. But for both of them, it is an extension of individual will and conscience—a perspective resonant not only with such nonconformist religious communities but with some of the mainstream American polity as well.

While the film is often read as an allegory for the Cold War, American isolationism, or the Red Scare, *High Noon* transcends these readings. Instead of only being classified as a timeless cinematic classic by generations of film scholars, the film offers us special access into the worldview of a specific time and place. Released in 1952, the geopolitical anxieties were prominent in the American psyche. Among these were the fear of Communist infiltration, the unease concerning the prospect of war with China, and the dread associated with the atomic bomb. But perhaps more important was not how these geopolitical factors helped popularize the view that *High Noon* operates mainly along allegorical lines, but that the film demonstrates the resilience of the cosmological presumption in relation to these anxieties. So while mechanistic time seems to irrevocably push the narrative (and history)

---

6. Hamm, *Quakers in America*, 47–49.

forward, suspense is perpetually sustained since without phenomenological knowledge we can never really know how events will specifically transpire. The cosmological presumption and the film's double preoccupation with its cinematic and chronological emblems demonstrate the concerns at work in the popular mentality of the time. These films show how loosely related anxieties cut across genre conventions of the time.

THE BIG CLOCK (1948)

In its intensity of double vision, John Farrow's 1948 suspense thriller *The Big Clock* surpasses the previously analyzed films. The trope of clocks as emblems of an orderly world pervades the film narratively and cinematically, and its overall preoccupation with time renders it an effective artifact of the cinematic cosmological presumption. In the film, Earl Janoth, the imperious head of a magazine conglomeration, oversees a multifaceted enterprise housed on several levels of a metropolitan building whose clocks are all perfectly synchronized with a master clock inside the building's infrastructure. Each clock is also synchronized with other clocks around the world. As a business leader, Janoth's characteristic managerial style is that of a horologist. Slavishly mechanistic, Janoth runs meetings by the minute, regularly giving subordinates "exactly one minute" to provide a plan to, for example, increase subscribers by ten thousand. The "big clock" manages its many workers on many levels: it ostensibly maintains their efficiency at work but also encroaches on their personal lives. This extreme chronological efficiency in exploiting different facets of human behavior was later satirized, for example, in Billy Wilder's *The Apartment* (1960), where the leaving times at work are staggered so as not to overcrowd the elevators and the liaisons using Baxter's home are scheduled so as to avoid the embarrassment of double-booking. When Janoth kills his mistress in her apartment with a sundial in a crime of passion, he turns to his protégé, George Stroud, to use his staff to track down the murderer, presumably to frame another person for the police. Since Stroud had also previously visited the same woman, Stroud tries to discover the identity of the real killer before he is incriminated by his own investigation.

The establishing shot prefigures the symbols and tropes that carry through the film. The image upon which the opening credits are cast is the sundial that will be used as the instrument of the woman's death. As one might expect, the opening musical score by Dimitri Tiomkin simulates the chiming of a clock as the credits roll over the sundial. The suspense device that sets its characters in pursuit (what Hitchcock termed the "MacGuffin") is thus conflated with a premodern form of chronometry. The premechanistic device used to show the movement of time and space is used to terminate the life of one of its characters.

The establishing shot then pans over a nocturnal city skyline and eventually tilts down, focusing on the ground-level window of the Janoth Building. It zooms into the interior where Stroud the protagonist hides from a security officer. His noir-style voice-over narration informs us that he is going to hide in the "big clock." The clock's sign in the lobby, flanked by sculptures of Atlas holding the Earth, reads "Friday/April 25/11:23." He reminisces about how things were different just thirty-six hours ago, at which time the clock's sign dissolves to thirty-six hours before. So in the opening shot the conflation of mechanistic time with global space is already firmly established. Later, we see that inside the clock is a massive rotating driveshaft which seems to visually refer to the *axis mundi* of early modern European attempts to demonstrate the geopolitical center of the world by associating the *axis mundi* with cosmic order.

When Janoth first appears, he proclaims that "there are 2,810,376,000 seconds"[7] in the average life span (of a ninety-year-old), admonishing his subordinates to use this time effectively on the job. Janoth's hard, deterministic managerial style simulates the hierarchical order of a mechanical cosmos. He often castigates subordinates about their duties, dictates by fiat, and even terminates his menial laborers for making minor mistakes. In pursuit of perfection, the hierarchical mandate to know one's place is enforced throughout the film. In his time imperium, Janoth even uses surveillance technologies to manage his employees. Using secret surveillance telecoms, he manages to wield almost totalitarian control over the Janoth enterprise. To be sure, the last third of the film occurs entirely inside the building, as Stroud struggles to escape the cordon of Janoth's security officers. The film's location and the inability of Stroud to inform the proper law enforcement authorities (due to evidence incriminating himself) create a kind of claustrophobic cinematic quality. Janoth's totalitarianism on the home front just three years after the war's end probably could have colored Janoth as a kind of crypto-Nazi reminiscent of Charles Rankin in Orson Welles's *The Stranger*.

Throughout the film, Janoth is identified as the embodiment of a mechanistic clock. He gives a wristwatch as a gift to the doorman, he makes a personal meeting at exactly 10:55, and he orders deadlines of minute-based times, as when he gives Stroud "six minutes" to decide if he wants to continue to work for him. Stroud muses privately, "I thought all [Janoth] is crazy about was clocks" to which Janoth's mistress retorts, "Maybe I have

---

7. Farrow, *Big Clock*, 0:08:50–0:08:55.

a clock."⁸ Janoth's mannerisms and demeanor simulate the regularity and composure of a mechanistic clock. But this regularity is punctuated in a moment of passion when his mistress goads him in private. Charles Laughton's performance of Janoth suggests a psychoanalytical rationale for his act. He sublimates his psychical energies like a machine until they eventually manifest themselves in a rare eruption of sexually tinged violence. In close up, Janoth reveals a dramatic facial tick that signals the fatal catharsis to come. The "tick" in this case is physiological, not chronometrical. Yet the pun is significant. This reference to psychoanalysis so typical of midcentury films resists the view that human behavior can be ultimately regulated by mechanistic time. By becoming the embodiment of mechanistic time, Janoth fatally denies his own humanity. In a final breakdown while attempting to elude capture, he falls to his death in his private elevator's shaft.

As Janoth is unable to perfect his living embodiment of mechanistic time, other characters evade the total orderliness of the clock/building apparatus. Unlike the other workers who labor purposefully on their appropriate floors and in their appropriate offices, Janoth's threateningly silent and nameless henchman seems to travel anywhere at will. He snoops around Stroud's office, enters surreptitiously through the building's back door and private elevator, and even explores the big clock in search of Stroud. He, too, eventually suffers his fate in the elevator shaft, presumably killed or captured as a result of transgressing the strictures of law and order.

In the murder scene, Janoth's mistress throws a mechanical clock at him in a rage just before he retaliates with the sundial. The violence associated with chronometers throughout the film is obvious. In addition to the repressive nature of the building's big clock, the sundial and the mechanical clock are both used as weapons, one of them as a bludgeoning tool. Janoth's armed henchman is knocked out by Stroud inside the clock itself, forcing his gun to fall to the floor. The clock's deadly associations are contrasted by the magazine's plan to increase subscribers by running a contest "promoting world peace." The world in 1948 was one certainly not free of violence, as millions of people continued to die of war-related injuries and diseases, not to mention subsequent violence characterizing the transmigrations of the nascent Cold War. Despite a decidedly violent geopolitical conflict waged in order to rescue democratic liberalism, world peace, like Stroud's security through most of the film, was tenuous and uncertain.

In fact, the totalitarian nature of the big clock's takeover of the film can be read as a critique of the flawed nation-state. Where the film begins by displaying diverse set pieces located outside the building (e.g., apartments,

---

8. Farrow, *Big Clock*, 0:17:10–0:17:15.

houses, bars) the film eventually denies Stroud and the viewer any access to the outside. Even Stroud's wife is consumed by the building's security dragnet. Characters who previously moved about with free agency have, by the end, been detained by the agents of the "big clock." Visitors to the building are even restricted from leaving, at least until the appropriate suspect is identified. But the viewer is also restricted from visualizing the authorities that lie beyond the boundaries of both the building and the mise-en-scène. In Hitchcockian manner, the possibility of Stroud's salvation by law enforcement agents is confronted and eliminated early in the film (since, based on circumstantial evidence, he would be the prime suspect of a capital case).

The threat of the state's monopoly on legitimate violence that Max Weber identifies is overwhelmed by the threat of the illegitimate violence represented by Janoth's pursuing henchman. The state seems entirely powerless to bring about justice. The film, which has been taken over by the big clock, oppresses those seeking justice in what appears superficially to be an orderly, mechanistic microcosm. In like manner, it is private citizens who do all the literal detective work in the film. Stroud and his several employees scour the city for clues and suspects. No authentic law enforcement officers are present in the film. Private security officers inside and outside the building maintain order, furthering the perception that the Janoth Building is a micro-state or a metropolitan version of a banana republic. A single police officer appears at the end—and actually turns out to be an impersonator.

The film's highly regulated setting becomes a simulacrum of an idealized state. Like the bureaucratic state, the business culture inside the building is a hierarchically structured meritocracy. Like the state, it uses the threat of violence to enforce civically appropriate behavior. Like modern institutions, it also appropriates the emblems of mechanistic time not only to function efficiently but to evoke a cosmological order that imbues its functions with enhanced authority. The Janoth microcosm is corrupt and uses these tools to protect the interests of the ruling clique rather than to uphold equal standards of justice for all its constituent members. It would seem the state can be characterized in a similar manner. Read this way, *The Big Clock* represents a critique of the nation-state in the midcentury period since, after the conclusion of the world's theretofore costliest global war, the most preeminent political authority in the world was the state itself. Interestingly, the investigative reporter, essentially a detective without police powers, was lionized in films like *The Big Clock* as well as others of the period like *Gentleman's Agreement* (1947), *Deadline USA* (1952), *Foreign Correspondent* (1940), and *Call Northside 777* (1948). These nongovernmental investigators share a familiarity with the protagonists of *All the President's*

Men (1976), whose Promethean knowledge helped expose and unravel a corrupt and paranoid presidency.

All of these examples, from the Disney animated features to *The Big Clock*, seem to point to a similar set of interrelated concerns in the midcentury period. They provide evidence that this double vision is present in other contemporaneous film traditions. Ultimately, identifying their resonant evocation of cosmic time helps locate the cosmological presumption squarely in the popular culture of the midcentury period.

Out of all midcentury suspense films, Alfred Hitchcock's *Shadow of a Doubt*, Orson Welles's *The Stranger*, and Carol Reed's *Odd Man Out* best exemplify the double vision that the cosmological presumption faced in this period of suspense and anxiety. They all deal self-reflexively with the emblems of time as order in the context of these unfolding developments in the geopolitical world and, perhaps more importantly, in the way we view the cosmos itself. The suspense of temporality is discernible in these texts.

What is of particular interest is that these films were made during one of the most serious crises the modern, democratic, American-led West had ever witnessed. Given the mutability and instability of midcentury colonial networks upon which financial infrastructures depended, the existential, aesthetic, and scientific challenges to orthodox religious hegemony, and the new migration of massive numbers of exiles, immigrants, and émigrés, it would be an understatement to say that a worldview so rooted in a belief in order should have suffered a debilitation under such pressures. Yet, perhaps surprisingly, it seems to have experienced a resurgence instead. My thesis is that the cosmological presumption is an essential characteristic of these films because they manifest the double vision, or metachronic, technique. Exactly how these films achieve this during the midcentury crisis—and what was their significance—is precisely the focus of the rest of this book.

Chapter 2 analyzes the 1943 film *Shadow of a Doubt*, a film that is uniquely positioned to demonstrate the metachronic principle at work. This chapter examines the ways the film employs emblems of time and polyvalent mechanisms that point to cosmic order during the early months of America's involvement in WWII. Chapter 3 analyzes the 1946 film *The Stranger*, which highlights similarly resonant themes. The relationship between geopolitical context and emblems of time is analyzed, with attention given to residual anxieties about the global conflict against Nazism. Chapter 4 analyzes the 1947 film *Odd Man Out*. This chapter considers the relationship between emblems of time and postcolonial identities and perceptions in the early Cold War period. It also discusses the film's unique employment of politics and religion and its relation to microcosmic time and time imperium.

CHAPTER TWO

Shadow of a Doubt (1943)

By WWII, the cinematic experience itself reified watching cosmic time. If anything, the cosmological presumption underlying this experience found a resurgence during this global conflict. It became tenacious, aggressive, and ubiquitous. It became reinvigorated by the struggle. The polyvalence of the nation-state model and Judeo-Christian orthodoxies perpetuated the cosmological presumption in the face of what was framed as a Manichaean global war. Propaganda films of the 1930s and 1940s that reinforced the pro-war (state) messaging and reinforced the preference for religiously determined moral order (church) did so in a geopolitical context of violence and devastation, though interestingly the conflict was increasingly framed as a war not of order against chaos but of (good) order against (bad) order. What is crucial to the metachronic thesis is that not only the content of such films but the very nature of the cinematic experience itself creates a unique experience whereby its agents may watch cosmic time and thus promulgate its premises. Thus the cosmological presumption was reinscribed in a specifically modern context by a group of popular filmmakers, most famously by Alfred Hitchcock.

SALVIFIC ORDER

Alfred Hitchcock directed approximately one hundred hours of what he termed "pure cinema" over the course of a career that spanned fifty years. As an auteur operating within the studio system, he developed an assiduous work ethic, making his production shoots an exercise in mass production efficiency, enabling him to accomplish such a bounteous output of terror.

As the popularly proclaimed "Master of Suspense," he, arguably better than any other director, knew the importance of pacing and timing; both are integral to the success of comedy and suspense—the tools of his trade. He experimented with narrative length; his shortest film, *Bon Voyage* (1944), runs approximately twenty minutes, while his longest film, *North by Northwest* (1959), runs approximately two hours and twenty minutes. He often managed to take time out of his intense schedule for carousing and vacationing; for example, he and his wife Alma annually revisited their honeymoon site at St. Moritz, Switzerland. From an early age, as Hitchcock biographer Donald Spoto points out, Hitchcock's favorite pastime was memorizing train schedules.[1] What do all of these elements have in common? Time. As a professional, as an artist, and as a family man, the regulation of time was of prime importance to Alfred Hitchcock.

Alfred Hitchcock was also raised as a Christian. As Eric Rohmer and Claude Chabrol suggest, Hitchcock's work inherently contributed to Christian art of the twentieth century.[2] His corpus demonstrates concerns over the nature of good and evil, faith and belief, damnation and redemption, guilt and innocence, and countless other central themes that develop specifically out of his religious heritage. In Christian cosmology, these themes are predicated on the premise that the world, though sinful, was created as an orderly system or at least by an orderly God. Hitchcock was personally and artistically infatuated with order and time, and this infatuation, typical of the cosmological presumption, is tempered by Christian principles acquired in

1. Spoto, *Dark Side of Genius*, 20.
2. Rohmer and Chabrol, *First Forty-Four Films*.

his formative years. Hitchcock himself said, "I had a strict, religious upbringing . . . I don't think I can be labeled a Catholic artist, but it may be that one's early upbringing influences a man's life and guides his interests."[3]

Though this obsession with time and order is often attributed to his Englishness or his idiosyncratic character, I am attributing this predominantly to his worldview, which was fundamentally shaped by both Christian orthodoxy and modernity. The central metaphor that God, the divine clockmaker, created an ordered world is mirrored by Hitchcock's cameo appearance in *Rear Window* in which he is seen winding a clock. That emblematic clock metaphor is not irrelevant but rather supremely significant. His view of time is based on a specifically Christian interpretation of order. Unlike a deist worldview in which the Supreme Being is remote and impersonal, the perspectives that inform Hitchcock's work demonstrate a cosmos that is constructed on the principle that Christ represents the incarnation of God and the fulfillment of God's ancient promise of salvation. What will be demonstrated is that Hitchcock's use and manipulation of conceptual time is intimately connected with Christian principles of law and order as evidence of a broader cosmological presumption common in this period.

Any brief survey of Hitchcock's films reveals the thematic significance of time and order. The crux of *Sabotage* (1936) is a boy unwittingly carrying a secret time bomb across London that will likely detonate while he is carrying it, dramatically highlighted by intercutting with clocks and watches. In *Rope* (1948), the accelerating pace of the metronome agitates Philip's guilty conscience. In *Dial M for Murder* (1954), Tony's watch stops at a crucial moment pertaining to the murder of his wife. In *Notorious* (1946), the time left before Alicia's conspiracy is exposed is measured by how many champagne bottles are left to be consumed at the party. In 1957, Alfred Hitchcock directed one episode of the TV show *Suspicion* titled "Four O'Clock" in which a watchmaker constructs a time bomb. Even in his short *Bon Voyage* (1944), a watch helps determine the narrative resolution. Arguably, the link between time and the spiritual connotations of law and order are present in every one of Hitchcock's films. For example, in *Vertigo* (1958), *North by Northwest* (1959), and *The Birds* (1963), time is fundamentally linked with order and disorder. To be sure, time serves an undeniable expository function in all narrative films. Hitchcock's films, not unlike traditional Christian morality plays, explain that the created order has become disjointed and needs to be corrected, and this responsibility falls not only to the religious or civic institutions, but also to the individual residents of that creation. This is a central theme in orthodox Christian theology represented in such

---

3. Spoto, *Dark Side of Genius*, 15.

essential texts as the catechismal writings of the Roman Catholic Church and the confessional statements of most Protestant denominations.

Vertigo offers a variation on the same theme. The film contains the usual seemingly insignificant references to time, such as when Elster offers Scottie a drink, he responds by glancing at his wristwatch and commenting on how early in the day it is. Time is not an insignificant theme in *Vertigo*, nor is it without spiritual connotations. With *Vertigo*, we are offered a cosmology in which history permeates the present. Yet, time is linked with a moral order. For example, the countless and almost subliminal reminders of the heritage of Christian morality abound in the vistas of San Francisco and its surrounding environs. The name "San Francisco" obviously refers to Saint Francis, certainly one of the most famous Catholic moralists. Moreover, the church across from McKittrick's, Carlotta's grave in the churchyard, the crosses on the graves, the restored San Juan Bautista mission, the spire clearly visible in Midge's window, and the telephone pole that is cropped to resemble a cross outside Scottie's apartment during Scottie and Madeline's second meeting all serve as reminders of Christian history.

Interestingly, the most political signifiers are found in the most natural setting. In Muir Woods, outside of San Francisco, Scottie and Madeline look at time through a cross section cut through a once-living organism, a tree. "Sequoia," Scottie explains, means "always." What are found in the rings are reminders of political history, such as the Battle of Hastings in 1066 and the signing of the Declaration of Independence in 1776. Both the religious and political symbols serve as reminders of law and order in history; they both help us to orient ourselves within a more transcendent reality.

After the officer plummets to his death at the outset of the film, Scottie is troubled by guilt. After Madeline's death, Scottie is also tormented by guilt. This time, however, the guilt is derived from his lateness. Presumably, he seems to think, if he had caught her before she ran into the church, he could have saved her. This notion is reinforced by the court's harsh criticism of his sin of omission. Guilt—that is, the perception of one's own moral transgression—and time are interconnected. According to the doctrine of original sin, postlapsarian human beings are born into a state of sin—and therefore guilt—as a result of the fall by Adam and Eve. Scottie is paralyzed by his guilt over the fall of both the officer and Madeline.

By the end of the film however, Scottie has become convinced that he must be liberated from the past and his inherited responsibility. He reconstructs Madeline's persona and the events of the crime in order to be liberated. At the end of *Vertigo*, Scottie, in the church bell tower, exclaims, "too late." The lateness to which he refers analogizes the disordering of his orderly view of the world. It is significant that a nun, initially seen as a ghostly figure, arrives too late to save Madeline and is, quite probably, the figure that literally frightens her to death. In other words, the responsibility for Madeline that Scottie inherited (to which he refers by invoking a Chinese proverb that saving one's life results in responsibility) has been challenged. For what or whom is he really morally responsible? This spiritual crisis is perhaps the source of his most profound anxiety, and this anxiety is based on the view of time that Hitchcock constructs.

In *North by Northwest*, being on time represents the maintenance of law and order. Faithfully observing a schedule becomes the primary concern of the characters. The film is filled with references to times and locations—coordinates, as it were. Addresses, room numbers, destinations, appointments, time lines, itineraries, and other numbers fill the schedules of the busy and efficient characters portrayed in the film. Even a superficial viewing of the film reveals numerous subtle indications of time and speed: The *Twentieth Century* Limited, Mount *Rush*more, *Rapid* City, Central *Time*, and *rush hour*, not to mention the ubiquitous dialogical concerns over timeliness. "Roger, will you be home for dinner?"[4] Thornhill's mother asks while he is pursued by murderers. This is a world filled with clocks and schedules and the millions of people who observe them and those who do not. For instance, the establishing shots depict the multitudes of busy New York City people following conventions of time. The buses, taxis, cars, and crosswalks all run on the efficient regulation of time and space; the belief in a rational mathematical or geometric design underlies them all. This geometry, which is repeated throughout, is first indicated by the title sequence showing regular angles and a consistent set of intersecting lines. This abstraction transforms into the orthogonal lines of a city building. These buildings represent the attempt to create order or, in the case of Vandamm's Rapid City structure, to build onto the natural order.

A cursory glance reveals the ubiquitous specific representations of time throughout the film in dialogic, diegetic, and filmic terms. In terms of the mise-en-scène, in the initial kidnapping scene, the watch of one of the kidnappers is clearly in view as the other's gun is pointed at Thornhill's heart, linking the efficiency of time with the efficiency of death. At the train station in Chicago, the train worker convinces the authorities that he was mugged, though he is still clearly sporting a respectable watch. It is not difficult to notice the watch, since all of his clothes were ostensibly taken by Thornhill. At the same station, the clock is seen in the background over Thornhill's shoulder while obtaining directions from Eve. The presence of the clock, though it is subtle to the point of being missed entirely at the conscious

---

4. Hitchcock, *North by Northwest*, 0:34:00–0:34:05.

level, serves several functions. It provides the audience with information that will later become useful; she received her instructions from "Kaplan" at around 9:15, although he checked out of his hotel at 7:10. It also serves to link Thornhill visually with time, which is vital both to his life and vocation. It also reminds us of the almost imperceptible sense of orderliness that keeps the rest of the world from devolving into chaos. Later in the hospital, Thornhill is seen shirtless, wearing only a towel and his watch. Again, this serves many purposes, not the least of which is to remind us of the urgency of time and his intimate consciousness of being timely. After all, important government secrets, not to mention his new love, will quickly be leaving.

Running throughout the film are innumerable references to efficiency and inefficiency. For example, notice the specific instances of lateness in the dialogue and the narrative. One of the first lines of the film (appearing just after Hitchcock's cameo featuring lateness) indicates Thornhill's lateness for his meeting with business associates. His mother, a few minutes later, bemoans that she "will be late for the bridge club."[5] The professor, meeting Thornhill at the airport, admits "I thought I'd never make it."[6] Lateness is a supreme transgression in a world built on the strict observance of order.

If lateness is a transgression then stopping is certainly a threat possibly leading to doom. The train Roger and Eve are riding in makes an "unscheduled stop" that allows the authorities to board in pursuit. Having eluded the authorities, Thornhill makes his rendezvous with destiny the next day at "Prairie Stop." The stop is almost his final stop. The propellers of the crop duster sent to kill him seem to vaguely suggest the hands of a clock-turned-deadly-machine, not to maintain order, but to create death. While escaping from the hospital, Thornhill is stopped by a patient who twice orders him to stop. Had he stopped long, Eve and the state secrets may have left with Vandamm. Even at Vandamm's, the housekeeper keeps Thornhill "pinned down for five minutes" with a gun. When he tries to escape from her she shoots at him three times. In that scene, the time until Eve's doom (and the violation of American security) is measured out in luggage. By this time, Eve knows that when the luggage is gone, she will be as well. This echoes how Alicia's doom is measured by champagne bottles at the party in *Notorious*.

Such examples further link stopping or ending time with the potential for annihilation. For a director raised to believe in a worldview that includes an eschatology, this metaphor seems rather fundamental. Notice how Thornhill's most aggressive verbal threat specifically relates to his knowledge of Vandamm's itinerary, but is also tempered with spiritual overtones.

---

5. Hitchcock, *North by Northwest*, 0:29:05.
6. Hitchcock, *North by Northwest*, 1:36:32.

"Suppose I tell you," Thornhill asks, "I not only know the exact time you're leaving tonight, but the latitude and longitude of your rendezvous and your ultimate destination?"[7] What is Vandamm's *ultimate* destination going to be? There is the literal (some Communist nation, perhaps), the legal (imprisonment or execution), or the spiritual (eternal damnation in hell). It is not clear which one is intended, though the final "ultimate destination" may be supported by very subtle Christian ideology present in the film.

Throughout *The Birds* are also found the apparently ordinary references to time, but these are not entirely ordinary. For example, Mitch's neighbor at his San Francisco apartment tells Melanie that Mitch has gone away for a few days; implicit in his comment is the assumption that, if she leaves the two birds by his door over the weekend, they may die. It would be irresponsible of her to leave them and, in a small way, her action would disrupt the natural order—at least for the birds. Her moral obligation is intimately connected with time. Interestingly, *The Birds* begins with lateness and ends with eschatology. Melanie's order is late, she is told at the pet store. It is while she is contemplating this lateness that she meets Mitch, whom she spontaneously visits the next day; her visit to Bodega Bay is coincident with the revolt of the birds, which apparently leads to the end of human civilization.

Does it logically follow that the "end of the world," as the drunken prophet in the Bodega Bay diner calls it, will occur because Melanie's order was late? This is a difficult claim to make. Undeniably a connection exists. Melanie is that connection, a socialite infamous for her destabilizing influence. It is significant that Mitch's profession is the law, a rather obvious reference to human moral order. The number of lawyers present in Hitchcock's oeuvre is noteworthy, especially in relation to the connection between time and law and order; lawyers figure prominently in *North by Northwest*, but also *The Wrong Man* (1956), *Rebecca* (1940), *Strangers on a Train* (1951), and *The Paradine Case* (1947), as well as many other of his films. Mitch's legal-mindedness and rationality are demonstrated by his interrogation and verbal lawyer-like jibes towards Melanie in the pet shop and as she prepares to leave his home after dinner. It takes two hours to reach his home in Bodega Bay, Melanie is told by his neighbor early in the film; although they are separated by distance, their separation is described in chronological terms.

Perhaps more disturbing than any violent bird attacks in the narrative is what they represent to the established order. Apparently, the only effective way to combat the birds' onslaughts, which can seemingly occur at any and all times, is to organize. The construction of order is humanity's defense

---

7. Hitchcock, *North by Northwest*, 1:43:34–1:43:37.

against the end times. Futile though it may ultimately be in *The Birds*, humanity's solidarity and practical action, such as Mitch's barricading of his house, seem humanity's best hope in a crumbling, apocalyptic world. As Donald Spoto observes:

> Order was an important value in Cockney life and in the Hitchcock home, and death and war and financial uncertainty were breaking down that sense of order and replacing it with the sense of chaos and the omnipresent possibility of disaster. This became, with the years, an attitude toward life, and it is perhaps the single most obvious situation in Hitchcock's films—the sudden disruption of chaos and disorder into a life of apparent security, and the psychological and emotional reactions this eruption evokes.[8]

It is relevant that Hitchcock lived through a Europe destroyed by the Great War. His hometown of London was savagely bombed in the first several years of World War II. This represents another deadly threat from the sky that could descend at any time. It is important to keep in mind the apocalyptic idiom common to many modernist artists of this period, expressed in works such as T. S. Eliot's "The Waste Land" and William Butler Yeats's "The Second Coming." Many of them describe the breakdown of law and order in terms of the time-history metaphor. Christian eschatology is normally associated with a final separation of the guilty and innocent. Judgment day is only horrifying to those who have rebelled against God's order because it will bring everlasting damnation to them. Chaos is situated in the very cinematic experience itself, for "the chain of cause and effect that typically governs narration in the Hollywood cinema disintegrates after the first thirty minutes when, in the words of screenwriter Evan Hunter, 'a screwball comedy . . . gradually turns into stark terror.'"[9] The birds herald the end of human mastery of time and order.

Hitchcock's moral universe is predicated on an orderly system, human responsibility, the possibility for redemption, reinforcing faith with good works, and inherited guilt. In his corpus, such notions are manifested by the symbolic role of time. Saving time and keeping time therefore represent more than just observing a social nicety. They represent the maintenance of moral order, synonymous with cosmic order. Consequently, lateness represents more than just a faux pas. It represents a supreme transgression against the cosmological presumption. Often, it is causally associated with the threat of death and destruction. Perhaps nowhere in Hitchcock's work is this principle more poignant than in *Shadow of a Doubt*. In it, timeliness and lateness reflect the ideological presuppositions

---

8. Spoto, *Dark Side of Genius*, 30.
9. McCombe, "'Oh, I See . . .,'" 67.

of their creator, Alfred Hitchcock. This film and its related issues are the focus of the rest of this chapter.

THE MORAL IMPERATIVE

The historical context of the film *Shadow of a Doubt* is World War II. Notwithstanding a later deemphasizing of the moral binary oppositions of "good" and "evil" constructed by Allied propaganda, the notion that the Allies were fighting the "good war" implies an evil and permeated the popular culture of the period. The plethora of posters, songs, and films of the early 1940s implied the moral conditions for going to war and fighting for democratic ideals. This is evident in one of the most popular films of the period, Michael Curtiz's *Casablanca* (1943), which highlights the moral significance of Rick's heroic shift away from neutrality at the conclusion of the film. Indeed, after Congress declared war on December 8, 1941, America was involved in fighting a/the good war. Such was America's zeitgeist.

After his semipermanent exile to America in 1938, Alfred Hitchcock had felt, as had many European émigrés, a sense of responsibility to urge America to go to war against the Axis powers. The United States had maintained an official position of military neutrality since Congress's ratification of the Neutrality Act in 1937. Hitchcock, along with numerous Hollywood directors in the late 1930s and early 1940s, communicated these political convictions through the powerful medium of popular film. Fritz Lang, who had been despised by Hitler's regime after his exodus from Germany, was perhaps the most outspoken émigré director in this regard. Among the earnestly pro-war films of 1940 were Mervyn LeRoy's *Escape* and Frank Borzage's *The Mortal Storm*. Hitchcock's Oscar-nominated *Foreign Correspondent* (also produced and released in 1940) is his most overtly political of the officially neutral period, demonstrating the immediacy of the fascist threat in Europe from the ostensibly neutral perspective of a reporter. *Saboteur* (produced and released in 1942) and *Lifeboat* (released in 1943) both dealt with the ingenuity, tenacity, and danger of the enemy's threat; among the other thematic similarities is the need for acceptance of differences in forging a coalition capable of democratic victory.

He even directed two short propaganda films in 1944 celebrating the French Resistance, *Bon Voyage* and *Aventure Malgache*. They were shot in five weeks and were not released; the distributor apparently did not find them lucrative and did not release them. Many decades later, they were rediscovered and made available on videotape. Hitchcock undertook other artistic endeavors to promote the war cause, however, such as directing a

"Buy War Bonds" commercial for David O. Selznick.[10] Though Hitchcock is typically considered an apolitical director, these films, in addition to the anti-Communist *Torn Curtain* (1966) and *Topaz* (1968), demonstrate a particular political energy. There are any number of reasons why he chose such works, but it may not be apparent that the motivation for filming these "political" films may also stem from the religious cosmology based in identifying good and evil which he acquired during his formative years.

Although Donald Spoto claims, quite weakly, that he "played no substantial role in the war effort," he does suggest an important motivating factor for Hitchcock's psyche—guilt.[11] Hitchcock had not been present at the death of his father, mother, or brother. He had not served in either of the two world wars. He had indulged in numerous vices that would have been considered naughty by the strict standards of his Jesuit upbringing: overeating, excessive drinking, ribald humor, and gruesome practical joking, not to mention relishing a special iconic status in popular culture based largely on scaring people half to death. He maintained a regular but marginal association with the Catholic Church, arguably for the sake of his daughter, and apparently rejected the Catholicism that had been foisted on him from an early age; however, he never fully abandoned the influence of the Christian worldview. It became largely secularized and is reflected throughout his work. As America mobilized for war in early 1942, his personal guilt likely affected the production of his favorite film, *Shadow of a Doubt*, making the work an exceptional example of his perspective of the world, especially as it relates to time, order, and morality.

For Hitchcock, this was an unusually difficult time personally. The imperious and micromanaging David O. Selznick, the producer to whom he had been contractually yoked, proved to be a manic-depressive antithesis to Hitchcock's rational and methodical approach to directing; consequently, Hitchcock's working relationship with him through the decade was miserable. Hitchcock's business manager said that the infamous contract was "replete with provisions unfavorable to Hitchcock and advantageous to Selznick."[12] Just before *Shadow of a Doubt* began production in the spring of 1942, screenwriter Thornton Wilder, the Pulitzer prize-winning playwright, joined the army and was sent away from his work on the script.

As Wilder travelled to his deployment by train, Alfred Hitchcock and producer Jack Skirball rode with him, putting the finishing touches on the

---

10. Taylor, *Hitch*, 186.
11. Spoto, *Dark Side of Genius*, 266.
12. Leff, *Hitchcock and Selznick*, 35.

script.¹³ Of course, any serious proponent of auteur theory must concede the screenwriter's and even producer's major role in film production. Wilder's contributions were significant even for the prototypical directorial auteur like Orson Welles. Welles said that of Hitchcock's work, *Shadow of Doubt* is "the American movie I liked the most. It was the one Thornton Wilder wrote . . . Thornton's natural warmth was a big help. There's a certain icy calculation in a lot of Hitchcock's work that puts me off."¹⁴

In addition to these difficulties, Hitchcock received crushing news that his mother was dying in her home in England. She had been diagnosed with life-threatening kidney and intestinal ailments. She died on September 26 that year of pyelonephritis, an abdominal fistula, and intestinal perforation.¹⁵ By the spring of 1942, the German and Italian armed forces had advanced to claim the majority of the European continent. Travel to England was extremely treacherous and difficult to schedule at the time, so Hitchcock threw himself, reluctantly, into his work. Understandably, sacrificial responsibility was an overwhelming force for him at the time, as it was with America. Consequently, *Shadow of a Doubt* is tinged with the religious significance of pain and disillusionment.

The protagonist of *Shadow of a Doubt*, Charlie, is a bright high school graduate who is especially fond of her Uncle Charlie. The identical spelling of both characters' names (instead of masculine "Charley" and feminine "Charlie") links them in a way that is invisible to the audience but clear to those with access to the original screenplay. Several facsimiles of Wilder's original screenplay notes are printed in Dan Aulier's *Hitchcock's Notebooks* and demonstrate this subtle but significant difference. Charlie comes to suspect that her dashing, worldly uncle has murdered several women and is hiding from the law in her hometown. Teresa Wright was cast for the lead role of Charlie. Wright also starred in two home front films that won the Academy Award for Best Picture in the next few years: *Mrs. Miniver* (1942) and *The Best Years of Our Lives* (1946). Both films associate her directly with the personal sacrifices involved in fighting "the good war." The moral imperative understood among the Allies in World War II but only obliquely implied in *Shadow of a Doubt* is suggested very early in the film. The Newton family of Santa Rosa, California, represents a middle-class, nuclear family. Charlie, the eldest daughter and recent graduate, detects that the family is in desperate need of salvation. She assumes responsibility for saving her family and looks for a savior.

13. McGilligan, *Alfred Hitchcock*, 312.
14. Welles and Bogdanovich, *This Is Orson Welles*, 138.
15. Spoto, *Dark Side of Genius*, 260.

The exact nature of the imminent danger is uncertain. Her father even questions her identification of the problem. The vagueness of the threat may represent a form of the threat that is only slightly secularized. "I'm talking about souls," Charlie explains to her father, who still does not seem to understand (let alone seem inclined to confront) the peril facing his family, which, by all superficial standards, would not appear to be in need of saving. Mr. Newton does not detect this original threat and appears equally oblivious to the threat from the murderer living in his own house. Mrs. Newton remains oblivious to Uncle Charlie's threat even after Charlie almost dies in the garage; perhaps this is due to concern over being late for the lecture. What is the real threat that Charlie perceives? Scholar Elsie Michie suggests that the threat Charlie perceives is gendered by a specific historical context of patriarchal power.[16] Charlie, like her mother, may be doomed to endless drudgery and cut off from professional fulfillment in a traditional middle-class marriage of her own.

This is where identifying Hitchcock's use of the cosmological presupposition seems especially beneficial. The moral environment established in the opening shots presupposes a world determined by both order and chaos. The first shot of Ann Newton, Charlie's sister, shows her eating an apple. The apple, according to the Judeo-Christian heritage, suggests the central doctrine of original sin. Ann clearly does not represent Eve, but her symbolic function is to introduce the Christian iconography in a subtle and innocuous manner. Without being born into a state of sin and potential damnation, Christ's act of sacrificial salvation is meaningless at best. Also, in the opening shots of the Newton family house, Ann is seen reading *Ivanhoe*. The eponymous protagonist of Walter Scott's romantic novel par excellence is a Crusader demonstrating courage, faithfulness, and chivalry. *Ivanhoe* expresses the epitome of the moral imperative. The Crusades were represented in eleventh-century Christian propaganda as a cosmic fight of good against evil, not unlike the conflict between liberating armies of the Allies and the tyranny of fascism in the early 1940s. Original sin and Christian responsibility are thus subtly introduced through the seemingly perfunctory opening shots of the precocious daughter in the film.

Once the family comes together (father, mother, Ann, and Roger), the entire household rings with disorder. Overlapping dialogue, the type of which was pioneered by such films as Howard Hawks's *His Girl Friday* and Orson Welles's *Citizen Kane* in the previous couple of years, creates a cacophony of splintered conversations. Perhaps it is this disorder, symbolizing a greater spiritual disorder, from which Charlie believes the family should be saved.

16. Michie, "Unveiling Maternal Desires."

She mentally searches for a savior, admitting it would take "a miracle" to save them. Incidentally, this attention to the miraculous was not lost on the New Wave directors who helped fashion his status as an auteur in the 1950s. Jean-Luc Godard wrote in *Histoire(s) du Cinema* that Hitchcock was "the only one, apart from Dreyer, who knew how to film a miracle."[17] It is conceded that Charlie is not only highly intelligent—the top of her graduating class—but highly perceptive, even supernaturally so. Charlie apparently sensed Uncle Charlie's desire to visit from three thousand miles away and mentally "heard" the Merry Widow Waltz at the dinner table. The supernatural overtones of Charlie's perception cannot be easily dismissed within the logic of the film. In a moment of epiphany, she comes to believe her namesake to be that savior. Uncle Charlie and Jesus Christ are thus further linked. Notwithstanding the fact that he typically wrote for the stage, Thornton Wilder, would have had an eye for the words on the page, and, as the primary author of the script, could very well have influenced the inclusion of such a subtle association in the two names. Regardless, Charlie believes that order may be restored, and, because she has perceived the threat and identified the means to confront it, she must take action. It is the responsible thing to do.

Miracle or not, one of the few curious logical inconsistencies presented in *Shadow of a Doubt* is whether or not there exists in the world a degree of the supernatural. Recruiting the narrative logic of the film and the various clues provided by the mise-en-scène, a few questions likely emerge. How does Uncle Charlie evade the detectives in his Philadelphia neighborhood alleyway? Unlike Hooker's initially miraculous escape from a closed alley in *The Sting* (1973), in which the camera's slow close-up later explains that he descended into a drain, we are led to believe that Uncle Charlie has supernaturally levitated away from being apprehended. Neither the camera nor the script offers us any explicit clues as to how he elevated several floors in a few seconds. This mysterious power he may have is decidedly problematic for the narrative, because otherwise what is to stop him from flying away the next time he is pursued? Perhaps more curious is the aforementioned psychic communication between Charlie and her uncle.

In order to make sense of the logical rupture suggested by this inexplicable connection, we have at least two options. Either Charlie and her uncle experience a supernatural form of communication or they do not. The confusion is highlighted by the telegrapher's quizzical response to Charlie's possible claim to telepathy. The telegraphy/telepathy play on words offers us only ambiguity. Charlie herself does not know how to explain this inexplicable situation of her and her uncle simultaneously telegraphing each other.

---

17. Conrad, *Hitchcock Murders*, 46.

Is it possible that in this new world of general relativity and quantum physics they experienced simultaneity? Paradoxically, it is most probable that the improbable is the best explanation. In other words, the fact that they both acted on the same thoughts at the same time is probably a coincidence, although by that point in the film we have already been presented with the precedent of the inexplicable. Nonetheless, for Charlie, this coincidence, as is often the case, serves as confirmation of her own intuition concerning her duty to rectify the disorder. This is ironic, since Uncle Charlie's visit will ultimately undermine Charlie's cosmological presumption.

The spiritually tinged motivation to save others is found everywhere in Christendom, from Jesuit missionary projects to World War II. Mrs. Newton declares that helping the government census workers is the responsibility of the citizens. "It's our duty," she proclaims. "It's something the government wants."[18] This impulse to do good for others is typically inculcated in cultures that identify themselves as Christian. It is clear from the number of citizens who attend church that some motivation propels the citizens of Santa Rosa to participate in correct behavior.

The crusading moral imperative fueling America's nascent war effort is demonstrated by the near-absence of young men in the film. The only young man who is ostensibly the same age as Charlie is only referred to, is never seen, and is rejected outright by Charlie. It is conceivable that her rebuff, mediated by her friend Catherine, was due to the fact that he was not in fact serving in the military overseas. This reason is speculative, but serves as a probable explanation of Charlie's reaction. The next oldest eligible men were the servicemen seen in the Til Two Bar, enjoying some drinks while taking time off from their duty to the Armed Forces. Graham, perhaps a little older still, is also respecting his moral duty by hunting down a mass murderer for the government. Actor Macdonald Carey, who portrayed agent Graham, did so in between two war-related films in which he played military officers: *Wake Island* (1942) and *Salute for Three* (1943). This military typecast may have even tinged the character of Graham as a military or paramilitary agent of the government. In any case, Charlie has few romantic prospects specifically because of this environment of moral responsibility.

COMMUNITY CLOCKWORK

The Newton family happens to share their surname with Sir Isaac Newton, the famed Christian scientist and the progenitor of natural theology. Such a cosmology, as described earlier, rests squarely on the divine clockmaker

18. Hitchcock, *Shadow of a Doubt*, 0:37:04.

presupposition: if one finds a watch, it must be concluded that a clockmaker made it. If time is ordered then the universe is orderly. If the universe is orderly, then an orderly entity created it. Isaac Newton, known for reconciling some of the polyvalent religious and scientific frictions raging among late seventeenth-century intelligentsia, explained the universal order in clear, rational, and understandable principles. The Newton family members—clearly intelligent, moral people—observe the conventions of orderliness and timeliness; it is fitting that Mr. Newton receives a wristwatch as a present. He displays it proudly and comments on it. The clockwork universe explained in natural theology and popularized by Newton is thus introduced in a subtle, albeit significant, manner.

In the 1940s, the Newtonian cosmological model was in the process of paradigm-shifting. Most frontier physicists had just begun incorporating relativity and quantum into their cosmologies, but these had yet to "trickle down" into popular usage. Newton's quasi-religious descriptions of the universe's orderliness must have provided much comfort to orthodoxies of church, state, and science, not to mention the commonplace world. His model operated out of the cosmological presumption that the Judeo-Christian God created the cosmos in an orderly fashion. Scientists gifted enough to comprehend the physical laws of the universe could know the mind of God. This theistic premise, of course, runs through much religious imagery, but also that of modern statecraft, as identified by Robert Bellah's analysis of John F. Kennedy's inaugural.[19] Modern scientists operate out of a parallel presumption that physical laws are universal, and therefore have a particular orderliness to them usually insofar as they regulate the structures of material reality.

Newton is probably best remembered by laymen of today for his elegant work on gravitational forces, explained in his 1687 *Principia Mathematica*. Part of this work includes a scientific explanation of absolute time. According to the Newtonian cosmology, time is homogenous. It is everywhere the same. All units of time are identical no matter where or when in the universe they are. In other words, absolute time is "time with nothing happening in it."[20] At the beginning of *Shadow of a Doubt*, the Newton family household, despite the overlapping dialogue, is uneventful. It is as if time in Charlie's home was a constant with nothing in it. Perhaps the reasons for the Newtonian model's appeal and tenacity is due mainly to its reductive mechanics. Presumably the entire universe is reducible to relatively simple physical rules that we can apprehend here on Earth. Both time and space can be quickly

---

19. Bellah, "Civil Religion in America."
20. Lacey, *Bergson*, 66.

understood by looking at a cosmic model like an orrery. The first modern orrery was commissioned by Charles Boyle, the eponymous Earl of Orrery in 1704, less than twenty years after Newton's *Principia* was published. The orrery shows in three dimensions the movements of the heavenly bodies relative to each other. It allows a viewer to see time as cosmic order.

Not unlike components of an orrery, the citizens of Santa Rosa move about in predictable manners, motivated by a sophisticated community clockwork. These kinds of orderly civic behaviors represented by this seemingly comprehensive community were later critiqued in the 1956 film *Storm Center*. This controversial film of the midcentury period about book burning and Communist hysteria was also filmed (although not set) in Santa Rosa, California, and dramatizes the negative effects of coercive conformity. In it, autonomous agency is replaced by an infectious desire to control the potentially destabilizing influences of knowledge in a middle-class community. The film here offers us an iteration of Charlie's Santa Rosa, inscribed into a Cold War milieu. In other words, although *Storm Center* is only tangentially associated with Hitchcock's film, we may use it as a measure of degrees of Santa Rosa's conformity in the midcentury period. Charlie's community is largely uneventful and predictable, two concomitant results of knowing the mind of God by perceiving his imprint of order in the world.

In discerning the moral environment of the film, it is also important to notice the history of Christian hegemony in Californian communities. Except for the opening scene of Uncle Charlie, the film takes place entirely in Santa Rosa, California. There seems to be significance in the name, for Uncle Charlie mentions it twice. "Santa Rosa. Santa Rosa, California,"[21] he tells the telegraph operator. Saint Rose was the first native from the Americas—indeed from the Western Hemisphere—to be canonized by the Roman Catholic Church. Like San Juan Bautista in *Vertigo*, San Francisco in *The Birds*, and Los Angeles in *Psycho*, these toponyms remind us of the presence of Christian settlement in America centuries earlier. Uncle Charlie also mentions his childhood home: Saint Paul, Minnesota. He later quotes Saint Paul by saying "Take a little wine for thy stomach's sake." The passage, taken from 1 Timothy 5:23, is significant because it marks the second time he invokes not only the name but the title of Saint Paul. Paul, of course, was perhaps the single most influential propagator of the Christian message, with the exception of the writers of the Gospels. His evangelism, a history of Christian expansionism, and Christian hagiography are all suggested by such references in the film.

Since names are always significant, Mr. Newton's Christian name, Joseph, seems to have been chosen intentionally as well. He shares his name

---

21. Hitchcock, *Shadow of a Doubt*, 0:07:08–0:07:11.

with the father of the Holy Family. As benign and loving head of the family, he represents the patriarchal hegemony that so dominated the major institutions of the 1940s. The family under his leadership uses his bank and goes to church on Sunday. The community of Santa Rosa seems to attend church without question. Outsiders—for example, the agents and Uncle Charlie—are shown clearly not attending church on Sunday, accentuating the compliance of those who do attend. For a film that initially appears to be about a family and a murderer, it contains numerous unmistakable references to a Christian worldview and cosmic time.

Peter Conrad, like many scholars whose work may reflect certain tacit agnostic positions, chooses to view Hitchcock's worldview as a harsh indictment of God at best and a proclamation that God does not exist at worst. From *Strangers on a Train*, he confusedly takes Guy's immoral and nihilistic antagonism as evidence of Hitchcock's personal views. Conrad argues, "Hitchcock inserted a barbed comment on a deity who enjoys the pointless, sportive fracas of nature."[22] Conrad then proceeds to discount constructive views of Christianity represented in his films. He even attempts to discount Hitchcock's own published words on the subject, endangering Conrad's credibility. Robin Wood writes, "His Catholicism is in reality the lingering on in his work of the darker aspects of Catholic mythology: Hell without Heaven."[23] Again, this view seems to ignore Hitchcock's own view that God exists whether or not we choose to believe. Divine justice will occur whether or not we believe it.

Shadow of a Doubt represents a world clearly associated with a moral universe of law and order. Santa Rosa is an ordered, idyllic community par excellence. The worldly institutions that permeate the town are structured on the presupposition of orderliness. The church, as an institution, derives its moral authority from the faith that the transcendent and orderly God has invested it with a spiritual mandate of salvation and integrity. The bank, as an institution, is based on consumer confidence. The motto "in God we trust" may be axiomatic, but the value of currency is derived from the commonly held belief that it indeed has value; it is important to note the several war bond advertisements at Mr. Newton's bank. Patriotism, the belief that America was fighting a "good war," and the stability of national security are neither discussed nor challenged—they are unironically assumed. The social structure maintains an aura of permanence, reflecting the particularly WASP-ish Great Chain of Being paradigm; men and women, young and old, rich and poor, white and black, outsiders and residents all have their preordained social places. All of

---

22. Conrad, *Hitchcock Murders*, 43.
23. Wood, *Hitchcock's Films Revisited*, 198.

these ideological state apparatuses reinforce each other's orderliness at a time when the modern world faced its greatest moral catastrophe in World War II.

Emblematic of this conflation of institutions is the clock tower in the center of town. The Bank of America building is seen in the background of several shots throughout the film and the clock tower juts above the Bank of America sign atop the structure. Like the Angelus of Roman Catholic tradition, the bell tolls to help regulate the behaviors of the community residents. In many small towns in early modern Europe, the Angelus clock tower would signify when to say the prayer in memory of Jesus Christ's assumption of his human form. It would typically be rung once in the morning, once at noon and once in the evening. In Santa Rosa, the bell has been modified from regulating community behavior for spiritual reasons to regulating behavior for other reasons less unified in purpose. It is significant that this regulatory machine is structurally attached to that most prominent economic institution—the bank.

Scattered along the interior walls of the bank are posters promoting war bonds. As Uncle Charlie visits Mr. Newton at the bank, this propaganda is seen in the background, suggesting the association between purchasing and patriotism. To reinforce this, the flag is visible near the roof of the bank. The message seems to imply that, in order to support the soldiers who are fighting for freedom, it is important to invest in the capitalist economy. Uncle Charlie evidently does not invest in any, which potentially characterizes him as somewhat less than a patriotic American. The economy, the government, the church, and the family all run like clockwork, regulated by time and timekeeping devices. The threat of disorder that Charlie discerns in her own family is a microcosm of the global disorder facing the external world.

CITIZENS ON PATROL

Uncle Charlie does manage to embarrass his brother-in-law among his boss and co-workers at the Bank of America. Making a bad joke about smuggling and hinting that Mr. Newton would someday have his boss's job, he seems to make everyone present uncomfortable. Charlie scolds him. "Uncle Charlie, you're awful. Everyone can hear you!"[24] she exclaims in surprise, shifting her previous tone when she proudly declaimed, "I want everyone to see you!"[25] on the way to the bank. Seeing and hearing, as well as overseeing and overhearing, figure strongly in Hitchcock's collection of themes. Perhaps inherited from his working-class London neighborhood, Catholic school, or simply cultivated as an adult for other reasons, the relationship between surveillance and appropriateness in his films seems to be an especially salient theme. Agent Graham says of the world, "Sometimes it needs a lot of watching. It seems to go crazy every now and then."[26]

In Santa Rosa, the motivation for such community surveillance is to maintain propriety and, by extension, law and order. Consequently, Charlie's indiscretions become supreme transgressions. From Mrs. Newton, who offers gentle admonitions, to Catherine, who stares disapprovingly, the citizens of Santa Rosa are all citizens on patrol. It is important to note the negative effect that Uncle Charlie has on his niece by the way this is exhibited to the community standards of propriety. Charlie lies to Catherine that she is ill and cannot go to the movies with her. Fifteen seconds later in the film, Catherine discovers her strolling with Uncle Charlie. Charlie is caught in a blatant lie and, seconds later, has a good laugh about it with her uncle.

Subsequently, Charlie lies to her family about Uncle Charlie, to Graham about what she knows, and, presumably, to her community about Uncle Charlie's evil. She and the church share complicity in promulgating the ultimate lie that Uncle Charlie was a decent person. "The beauty of their souls, the sweetness of their characters, live on with us forever,"[27] a speaker at Uncle Charlie's funeral service says about him. This lying is clearly done for the sake of her family and community. The law enforcement agents, representing the institution of the government, also share the responsibility for this cover-up. Ultimately, Charlie becomes a liar for the sake of others. For one who believes in the importance of morality, this is a sacrifice.

24. Hitchcock, *Shadow of a Doubt*, 0:40:19–0:40:21.
25. Hitchcock, *Shadow of a Doubt*, 0:39:34.
26. Hitchcock, *Shadow of a Doubt*, 1:47:30–1:47:35.
27. Hitchcock, *Shadow of a Doubt*, 1:47:40–1:47:45.

The traffic officer, a professional citizen on patrol, is perhaps the most significant figurehead of this time metaphor. Employed to regulate order, the officer makes four symbolically important appearances in the film. Framed in the first three appearances with the Bank of America clock tower visible in the background, he obviously represents the maintenance of law and order. As the first citizen seen in Santa Rosa, his appearance mediates the viewer's entry into this community. The low-angle shot framing him with the clock tower accentuates his significance in the community. He is vigilant and powerful, though ineffective at detecting Uncle Charlie's true identity. Without the traffic officer, perhaps fatal accidents will occur. To reinforce this danger, Mr. Newton jumps to the conclusion that Aunt Sarah, having recently obtained her driver's license, has gotten into an accident. For Hitchcock, who rarely drove (except to church on Sundays), the fear of a horrible automobile accident may have been very real indeed.

For Charlie, three notable transgressions reveal a sinister and diabolical netherworld that subverts Santa Rosa's (and the universe's) order. Her visit to the library, the bar, and the train are all oriented in a time-order metaphor. In his article "All in the Family: Alfred Hitchcock's *Shadow of a Doubt*," James McLaughlin also deals with the association between time and law and order. While we agree on many points, he places this association in a context of Charlie's sexuality when it may more effectively be placed within Hitchcock's spiritual paradigm. Characteristically, McLaughlin states "One significant feature of the Law and Order that Charlie's phallicness threatens is the order of Time. . . . Sleep puts to sleep the time machine."[28] Charlie's "sins" are contextualized not only in terms of the community, but in terms of time as well.

Charlie, believing that she should learn something about Uncle Charlie by reading it in the newspaper, goes to the library. It is late. On her way there, the traffic officer stops her from crossing the street when she should not have. He makes her go back to the curb to wait for his signal, along with everyone else. Furthermore, when she is finally signaled across, he grabs her and scolds her for her impatience. Why? In the film's narrative, the transgression is associated with the danger of injury or death. But symbolically, in an orderly society, not conforming one's schedule to that of the authorities can lead to a breakdown of the system. The officer's reprimand links this violation of schedule with immorality.

As she speeds to the library, she notices she is too late and the library is closing. It is 9:00 at night. She pleads to be let in, to have some authority allow her transgression. While knocking on the front door, she receives

---

28. McLaughlin, "All in the Family," 150.

disapproving looks from citizens passing by, reminding us of the social pressures that reinforce the orderly system. It is easy to see the librarian, who explains "If I make one exception, I'll have to make a thousand," as a prickly stereotype. However, in this universal context, her symbolic function in the narrative is entirely consistent. It is her moral responsibility to keep to the preordained schedule. "You have all day," the librarian tells Charlie, visibly upset that she has violated her own duty. As a result of being given a reprieve of "just three minutes,"[29] Charlie finds the newspaper and learns about her uncle's supreme transgression—murder. These extra three minutes have entirely changed Charlie's view of the world and its established order.

After Charlie becomes upset at the murderous dinner talk between Herb and her father and leaves, Uncle Charlie, who has followed her, persuades her to visit a bar. On their way there, Charlie again runs into the ubiquitous traffic officer who benevolently warns that he may have to give her "a ticket for speeding." Uncle Charlie replies that they "don't want to break the law."[30] It is after hours in her world, but Uncle Charlie exposes her to a place that stays open late. The Til Two Bar, as advertised by clocks on the doors, represents a foreign world to Charlie, who is not used to the morally questionable activity that transpires there. The implication of moral degeneracy, indicated by the rowdy and perhaps drunken servicemen carousing with ladies, is directly associated with time. Louise, the bedraggled waitress, states that she has worked at the dive for "two weeks"[31] and apologizes for her tardiness. "Sorry I was so long."[32] Moreover, she admits that she "never" would have expected to see Charlie at such a place. It is within this context that Charlie hears her uncle's anti-sermon about his horrifying moral universe. Consequently, her life is changed forever. Like her uncle, Charlie has been transported out of time, and therefore, out of the established order.

This kind of *demi-monde* where people exist seemingly outside of the established order evolved rather curiously as a result of modernization. Western urbanization really began to dramatically increase at the beginning of the nineteenth century. Numerous scholarly sources trace the various socioeconomic push-pull factors leading to de-ruralization and urban population swells over the century. These trends appear strongly and perhaps even inextricably linked to industrialization. As social historian Roger Ekirch observes, "natural"[33] sleep biorhythms were largely obstructed by the

29. Hitchcock, *Shadow of a Doubt*, 0:59:30–0:59:50.
30. Hitchcock, *Shadow of a Doubt*, 1:01:13–1:01:20.
31. Hitchcock, *Shadow of a Doubt*, 1:02:12.
32. Hitchcock, *Shadow of a Doubt*, 1:04:33.
33. Ekirch, *At Day's Close*, 326–27.

mechanistic time that is the lifeblood of industrialization. Comparing sleep habits in premodern popular culture with those in the fullness of modernization reveals a host of psycho-social problems related to sleep deprivation. The modern epidemic of sleep loss, along with long-term concomitant ailments and hazards, has effectively been created by a forced communal conformity to the standard eight-hour industrial workday.

Charlie's typical world, though mechanistic, is hardly filled with anxiety. In fact, it appears idyllic. At least this is true at first glance. The out-of-time state she experiences with Uncle Charlie is presaged by her earlier sleeplessness. Soon after she has a "shadow of a doubt" about her uncle, she presumably stays up too late and sleeps in much later than usual. By reverting to her primitive circadian rhythms, she reasserts her identity vis-à-vis her temporal environment. Sleep is often culturally read as a passive experience but, as most modern cognitive and psychoanalytic research shows, sleep is active and even assertive. After learning the most disturbing news of her life, Charlie reacts in perhaps the most natural way—by reorienting herself in time.

Charlie's late night evokes the premodern and ancient regimentation of night intervals, before mechanical clocks. The Romans termed the period between midnight and the crowing of the rooster *intempesta*, or "without time."[34] This *intempesta* was typically considered the most dangerous, particularly because it was the most obscure. That is, sinister events could not only occur under cover of anonymity in the city, but under cover of darkness as well. This correlation reinforced the familiar trope of darkness as evil. Light proved one of the remedies to the dangers of the *intempesta*. Improved urban lighting and curfews, first introduced on a large scale in Netherlands in the seventeenth century, discouraged criminally destabilizing behavior by exposing it to the communal gaze. By the 1940s, all major cities had sophisticated urban lighting systems to extend productivity temporally into the night but also to discourage members of the *demi-monde* from violating the established order.

The *demi-monde* that occurred alongside industrialization and urbanization thrived on one of the defining characteristics of urban life: anonymity. Being anonymous is as old as the city itself. But the dramatic wide-scale increase of urban populations made anonymity ubiquitous. The growth of the underworld, with all the related developments, such as organized crime, black market economies, human trafficking, and prostitution, while preexisting the modern age, was normalized due to the hundreds of new urban centers that sprang up around the West throughout the modern period. The

---

34. Ekirch, *At Day's Close*, 138.

challenges that criminal culture posed to an orderly society were met by several civic measures. The most emblematic antidote has been the growth of professional police forces. The emergence of these paramilitary groups, professionally trained and solemnized to enforce the laws, represents an historical shift in the nineteenth century. Again, police forces preexisted the modern period, but their ubiquity and special authorization in the liberal state made them part of the ideological state apparatus like never before. Since the professionalization of police forces, citizens took on a dichotomous role concerning surveillance. On the one hand, to be a citizen invested in the community, one needs to watch over their interests. But, on the other hand, authorizing and paying a group of professionals alleviated citizens of their direct civic responsibility to act as agents in maintaining order. After all, in America cops have come to been identified as citizens on patrol. Hitchcock expressed his ambivalence towards police officers throughout his corpus and in numerous colorful interviews.

The brief, final scene of his procession and funeral is permeated with a communal order. The procession snakes its way through a docile, orderly community in the shadow of the clock tower, the church minister ameliorates the mourning congregation with platitudes, and Graham patronizes Charlie's intelligence by telling her, in essence, everything will be fine. After the disorder of Uncle Charlie's accidental death, the community intuitively attempts to restore order. For the residents of Santa Rosa, this means a life of going to church, supporting the economy, and observing the laws—all with divinely inspired regulation.

MISSING THE TRAIN

As the Newton family prepares to send off Uncle Charlie at the train station, they are reminded of the lateness threat. Herb's warning "Here comes the train" implies "Don't be late or you'll miss it." What Herb does not know is that, if Uncle Charlie is indeed late, the avuncular menace will continue in Santa Rosa. Uncle Charlie lures Charlie onto the train in order to kill her. She is not able to leave the train before it starts. Again, lateness is associated with death and disorder. "Not yet, Charlie," Uncle Charlie says, clearly threatening to kill her as she tries to get off the accelerating train. As a result, Charlie struggles and indirectly brings about the horrific death of her uncle. Violating the orderly standards of time, once again, is linked with death, disorder, or disillusionment. Hitchcock's cameo on the train (one of several spread across his oeuvre) shows him playing cards with a physician. The train that brings Uncle Charlie's menace to Santa Rosa also conveys the director. In a supernatural stroke of luck or a masterful demonstration of expert cheating, Hitchcock is holding all the cards of one suit. The director, through his special powers, has allowed evil to come to town.

The medium of that infiltration is specific and emblematic. As economic historian Alfred Chandler observes, railroad and telegraph companies were the first real modern business organizations in that they standardized services for national distribution, employed professionals to coordinate these activities, and applied timescales and technologies in service of a centralized vision.[35] The central role of the railroad industry (along with its tandem telecommunication technology) in modern Western expansionism cannot be overemphasized. In remote areas of Britain and America, the railroad was the single most important civilizing organization. The facets of standardization, coordination, and chronometry that Chandler identifies overlaid this wide-scale civilizing experience with a decidedly modern dimension. As world-systems analysts would say, the railroad industry played a crucial role in the incorporation of the periphery into the capitalist world-system, forever changing the relationship of the frontier to the nuclei of industrialization.

It was the train that connected small towns with the wider world in its most material ways. Most notably transporting goods, technologies, and people, it was perhaps the most significant driving force in the mass implementation of the principle of manifest destiny. It allowed for the abrupt creation and destruction of communities along the frontier. As social historian Kenneth Jackson observes, many small village railroad stops like Santa Rosa had existed in isolation from major cities until the unprecedented railway expansion in the late nineteenth century, an expansion that "dissolved the barriers of time and distance to bring them into a more metropolitan orbit."[36] Before unitary train time was adopted in 1883, dozens of cities across the American West operated according to their own local "sun" time, which varied by increments of minutes between what would become the four continental time zones separated by single hours.[37] It was the train industry that incorporated small towns and cities across America into a standard national temporal-spatial system. We are reminded of this fact by the important role that trains play in this film, as in others directed by Hitchcock.

Because the modern railroad systems were enormously complex, technological, and sensitive to the preservation of their cargo, they especially relied on conventions of the new mechanistic time. In addition to

35. Chandler, *Visible Hand*.
36. Jackson, *Crabgrass Frontier*, 91.
37. Galison, *Einstein's Clocks*, 124.

the significant fact that it is the train that conveys Uncle Charlie to Santa Rosa, the train signals a mode of transportation that was intrinsic to the industrialization of all aspects of modern life by the 1940s. For example, the wartime home front setting of the film is again significant here. Since at least the late nineteenth century, trains became central concerns of war planning, mobilization, and implementation. As military historian Arden Bucholz writes of modern war before the adoption of mechanistic time in the late nineteenth century:

> There was no sense of timing. During mobilization the civilian train system fit nearly half a million soldiers slowly and intermittently into its normal timetable. The men were lucky to find their regiments at all: their orders were delivered by post or by local officials on horseback. Some officers received their orders five days after mobilization was declared.[38]

Five days after mobilization was declared simply would not do for modern war maneuvers that are calculated not just to the day, but to the hour and minute. In both world wars, trains moved inestimable amounts of material, food, and supplies, not to mention tens of millions of troops and civilians. During wartime, the train became an iconic representation of the movement of violence over the earth.

Whether carrying soldiers or victims of genocide, war trains represented a visual and aural reminder of the suspense of temporality, so characteristic of the filmic double vision. Not surprisingly, several traditional war films have appropriated (and perhaps exposed) the cinematic use of clocks and watches to regulate or measure combat. Set against great carnage, combat films as disparate as *The Longest Day* (1962), *Gallipoli* (1981), and *The Big Red One* (1980) have used this to great effect.

In this context, being late does not simply mark a social taboo, but a potentially traitorous activity. Consider the potential devastation if, during the war, timetables were altered in error or train tracks carrying sensitive cargo were disturbed. Likewise, the retaliation against a transgressor of the war train-time system could be harsh and fatal, likely resulting in execution. Being out of sync with the train schedule could mean death (as in the case of Uncle Charlie) but could also mean an even greater transgression against nation or God. After all, the world of wartime Santa Rosa and all other similar communities across America was one regulated by the cosmological presumption.

One of the champions of the cosmological presumption's moral imperative and salvific order is Herb, another unofficial citizen on patrol and Charlie's neighbor. Herb is also strongly associated with time. It is noted

---

38. Bucholz, *Moltke, Schlieffen*, 38.

that he comes earlier and earlier to the Newtons' home, often infringing on their dinnertime. He seems not to observe this mild infraction on their private time. Of all the characters, Herb is the one who actually saves Charlie from asphyxiation, though he is given little credit for this feat. It must be remembered that the observation about the oncoming train is uttered by Charlie's real-life savior, Herb. It is vital—supremely significant, even—to listen to his warning. By comparison, Agent Graham, Charlie's would-be savior, is impossible to contact when she needs him most. After Uncle Charlie's almost successful attempt at murdering her while the others are at the lecture, Charlie tries to contact Graham by phone numerous times. None of the attempts are successful. Graham's absence leaves Charlie to fend for herself against a mass murderer. Herb, seemingly by serendipity, is the one who saves her life.

The agents have been associated with time as well. In an earlier scene, posing as census workers, Graham and Saunders had arrived early at the Newton house, causing a great deal of turmoil for Mrs. Newton, who was unprepared for their visit. She had gone to lengths to remind Charlie not to be late for their 4:00 arrival, only to be frustrated when the agents violated their own schedule. Charlie lashes out at their intrusive attempts on their privacy, perhaps justified in part by their seemingly careless earliness. "When someone asks for privacy, they should have it."[39] When Saunders wants to take a photograph of Mrs. Newton breaking an egg for a cake, she sternly informs him that one cannot make a proper cake out of sequence. Their presence has caused a great deal of disorder in their household.

As Charlie shows Graham the upstairs, the grandfather clock is seen prominently between them. In a medium shot, they stand on either side of the frame, allowing the clock to mediate their conversation. Soon, Graham asks her on a date. They agree to meet at half past six that evening. They walk around the town and seem to have a good time. With her powers of perception, Charlie sees through his deception and is angered. They argue. When he rises to explain, the Bank of America clock tower appears, framed over his shoulder, visually reestablishing him with the conflation of institutions for which Charlie feels moral responsibility. In an unsettling platonic twist, the film seems to suggest that although Graham may have lied, he did it for the good of the community.

The agents try to force a time line on Charlie. After lying to her about their mission, they all but blackmail her into helping them. Saunders offers to postpone Uncle Charlie's arrest until Charlie can get him out of town. They give her a couple of hours. Uncle Charlie also manipulates her time

---

39. Hitchcock, *Shadow of a Doubt*, 0:45:20.

line, waffling about staying or going. "When are you leaving?"[40] Charlie asks him forcibly. The emphasis is not on whether or not he will in fact leave, but on what time he will leave. Both parties pressure her to conform to their schedule. It is the vocabulary of order. This identification between scheduling and death is evident even in the newspaper article exposing the Merry Widow Murderer. In the paper, Uncle Charlie's most recent victim is identified first by the date of her death—not her name. The article reads, "His latest victim, on January 12th, in Gloucester, Mass., was Mrs. Bruce Matthewson."[41]

This identification by time runs throughout the film. In the film's opening scene, Uncle Charlie is seen in bed, resting in the middle of the day. Later, in Santa Rosa, he gets up late and has breakfast in bed at 10:30. Mrs. Newton notes how he must be the only one in her community to sleep in so late. Sloth is one of the seven deadly sins of traditional Christendom. Santa Rosa represents an industrious society that eschews laziness. Mr. Newton, in his first conversation with Charlie, notes how work is one of the attributes of their community. Uncle Charlie has a schedule and agenda of his own, but he appears to others as one on a permanent vacation. Idle hands, it would seem, are the devil's playground.

In many ways, Charlie is linked with her uncle. She is linked by name, by blood, and by brain. She begins to lie like Uncle Charlie. This link is demonstrated, less obviously, by Charlie's sleeping time as well. The opening shot of her frames her on her bed in the exact posture as seen in her uncle's opening shot. After she reads in the newspaper of Uncle Charlie's latest murder, she sleeps in most of the next day—not unlike her uncle the previous day. While she sleeps, the diegetic bell from the clock tower tolls, aurally linking her with the community. This violation of the workaday world's schedule veers dangerously towards the sin of sloth.

She is also linked with him through the state of simultaneity. They apparently have been able to share thoughts over thousands of miles at the very same time. Charlie suggests that this may be due to telepathy, but what seems to be as remarkable is that the message was received instantly. What is most disillusioning for Charlie is that, by the end of the film, she realizes with whom or what she has really been intimately communicating. She has become complicit with his sins, and it has eternally made her an outsider in her own community. The verse from 1 Timothy 5:22, which precedes the one Uncle Charlie quotes at the Newton dinner table, warns, "Do not share in the sins of others. Keep yourself pure." The verse following Uncle Charlie's

---

40. Hitchcock, *Shadow of a Doubt*, 1:31:15.
41. Hitchcock, *Shadow of a Doubt*, 1:00:53.

quotation states, "The sins of some men are obvious, reaching the place of judgment ahead of them; the sins of others trail behind them. In the same way, good deeds are obvious, and even those that are not cannot be hidden." This seems to ultimately temper Uncle Charlie's deeds with an ironic sense of cosmic justice. Charlie has shared in the sins of Uncle Charlie and has become like him. It is significant that she rides the fateful train out of town along with her namesake. Metaphorically, she cannot go back. Her innocent life in Santa Rosa, like Adam and Eve's postlapsarian Eden, is forever irretrievable for her.

UNCLE CHARLIE, ANTICHRIST

Much has been made about Uncle Charlie's diabolical nature by other scholars. For example, Uncle Charlie is seen as a vampire by David Sterritt,[42] a devil with a sexual pathology by Robin Wood,[43] and an enforcer of patriarchal values by James McLaughlin.[44] He is clearly an antagonist, albeit a suave and charismatic one. To be sure, he is associated with both the devil and Dracula. Uncle Charlie eludes his pursuers in Philadelphia by seemingly and supernaturally flying up a building. He comes to town amidst a thick cloud of black smoke, carrying souvenirs of his sins. By the end of the film, Charlie comes to doubt that he indeed is the savior she summoned. The doubt suggested by the film's title refers to doubting her savior, who turns out to be demonic. He brings Charlie "nightmares." Ann has presumably read Bram Stoker's *Dracula* and is asked to tell the story. In the novel, published in 1897, Count Dracula represents a Victorian perversion or inversion of Christ. He drinks the blood of others, rather than having others drink his blood. His libidinous activity mocks Jesus's asceticism. His immortality is to be lived out on earth at the expense of others. Uncle Charlie is indeed an evil character. His skills include manipulation, seduction, and charisma. What is perhaps more intriguing is his identification as the antichrist.

Uncle Charlie proclaims his selfish personal philosophy throughout. "What's the use of looking backward?" he says. "What's the use of looking ahead? Today's the thing."[45] This is illustrated specifically with the vocabulary of time. The eternal present that he so admires creates the ideal state for an opportunist. He is free to go with Charlie on the town, to engage in business, or to leave at a moment's notice. He consequently exists in a

---

42. Sterritt, *Films of Alfred Hitchcock*.
43. Wood, *Hitchcock's Films Revisited*.
44. McLaughlin, "All in the Family."
45. Hitchcock, *Shadow of a Doubt*, 0:38:30.

perpetual state of anomie, free and unencumbered by moral responsibility. His duty seems to be to his own gratification. Perhaps perversely, he declares, "Heaven takes care of fools and scoundrels,"[46] shrugging off any anxiety over future events. What would be lauded as a *carpe diem* attitude by the Dionysians of the 1960s is identified in the 1940s as deviance in the atmosphere comprised of adult laborers driven by moral responsibilities to fight against evil. In other words, his cavalier perspective would be considered immoral and unpatriotic during the American war effort. Self-sacrifice is morally superior to self-aggrandizement, especially according to the prevalent zeitgeist of wartime Santa Rosa.

Uncle Charlie, the experienced traveller-businessman, explains the facts of life to Charlie as he understands them. "The world's a hell. What does it matter what happens in it?"[47] Uncle Charlie's logic would appear to be built on the following premises. The world we live in is filled with hellish horror and misery. Because the world is this way, we should question a morality that keeps us from gratification. What relevance do any of our actions have if we are subjected to such conditions? A world devoid of moral consequences creates a world without religion, which would seem to please Uncle Charlie. Instead of adhering to a traditional system of ethics, he lives by a perverted moral code—a perversion of Ivanhoe's Christian chivalry.

Murdering rich widows becomes his one passion in life. This type of malignant euthanasia, which figures prominently in Robert Siodmak's *The Spiral Staircase* (1945) and Hitchcock's *Rope* (1948), is neither truly Nietzschean nor utilitarian, but it is reminiscent of the genocidal justifications given for the Nazi programs of ethnic cleansing. To eliminate a people because they are inferior or represent a threat to one's way of life is genocide. To eliminate women because they inherit wealth and do not respect the work that went into earning it is psychopathic. Although the extent of Heinrich Himmler's "Final Solution" was not publicly known in 1942, the stated objectives of the Nazi regime were. Uncle Charlie's evil crusade to rid the world of these people seems the extent of misogyny, but it appears tame by comparison to the more nefarious developments in Europe. This moral ambiguity ("What does it matter?") mixed with a morbid sense of purpose—to kill widows—creates a paradoxical combination of motivating factors not foreign to the logic of the Holocaust. As early as *Mein Kampf* (1925), the Nazi project characterized their enemies, namely Jews, as vermin or animals. Uncle Charlie likewise dehumanizes his victims. "They're people, aren't they?" Charlie asks, shocked and outraged from off-screen.

---

46. Hitchcock, *Shadow of a Doubt*, 0:41:55–0:41:57.
47. Hitchcock, *Shadow of a Doubt*, 1:16:07–1:16:10.

"They're human beings!" To which Uncle Charlie asks, rather rhetorically, "Are they?"[48] This is one of the rare Hitchcockian subjective shots that engages the audience directly. Such an effect sometimes results in asking audience members to consider the cinematic experience or to consciously reflect on the statement. Whether a Nazi ideologue or demonic entity, he is certainly, in any event, the closest thing to the devil to live in Santa Rosa.

Certainly one of the most popularly demonized groups during America's counterattack against fascist aggression in WWII were the Nazis. Despite the popularity of American fascist movements and the large population of newly repatriated politically outspoken Germans in the years leading up to the Second World War, antipathy against German Nazis was recruited and fomented by official and nonofficial American propaganda by the time America entered the war. Perhaps the most sobering film images confirming America's moral superiority during the conflict came in the form of newsreels showing the devastating effects of the war on marginalized people inside the Third Reich. The newsreel reportage, showing emaciated survivors of the concentration camps or rows of corpses being bulldozed into mass graves, shocked American audiences in the wake of the war. Hitchcock himself was commissioned by the British government in 1945 to direct a full-length documentary film made from footage of the liberated camps. It included eight thousand feet of film, spanning eleven European concentration camps. After working on the film for a few months and viewing "all the film as it came in,"[49] Hitchcock resigned from the project, sickened and disgusted. The film was never made, but these types of postwar documentary films later inspired other films to focus on the transportation of genocide victims by railway. Among them, *Shoah* (1980), *Schindler's List* (1993), and *The Last Train* (2006) dramatize the iconic relationship between trains and the Holocaust. To be sure, such mass killing would not have been possible without the technical sophistication of mechanistic time in service of the state. In *Shadow of a Doubt*, the same kind of transportation (i.e., the train) that by 1945 would be associated with mass mobilization and mass extermination is associated with the movement of a killer into town and out of town to his own death.

Uncle Charlie's status as an antichrist is further portrayed by his perversion of one of the central Christian sacraments: marriage. He has apparently killed many single women in an act of twisted justice. Marital frustration-turned-murder is the source of morbid jokes and crime dramas for Hitchcock, but Uncle Charlie kills for a purpose. In a cruel mockery

48. Hitchcock, *Shadow of a Doubt*, 1:08:15–1:08:19.
49. McGilligan, *Alfred Hitchcock*, 373–74.

of the marriage sacrament, he consummates the bond by killing his mate. Throughout the film, he is identified by sexuality. He is handsome and experienced, Charlie and Catherine are clearly attracted to him, and he flirts with Mrs. Green at the bank. Perhaps more disturbing are the incestuous undertones of his relationship to Charlie and Ann. Charlie's attraction to her uncle has already been noted, but Ann's sudden plea to her mother before dinner suggests inappropriate relations. Ann, uncharacteristically pensive, secretly asks to sit away from Uncle Charlie at the table. The typically rational Ann appears somehow ineffably disturbed. Other than this explanation, Ann's behavior makes no sense. He represents a sexual threat to the young women of the Newton family, though this is never communicated verbally. In essence, the young women have had relations with the devil.

As Charlie returns from church, Uncle Charlie mocks such religiosity, joking that the show's been running so long he assumed the attendance had slipped. He does not attend church, further identifying him not only as an outsider but as the devil. The ultimate irony of his animus for God is that, in the final scene, his corpse is ostensibly brought into the church for the funeral service. Pious platitudes are spoken about his goodness inside, while Charlie, now standing outside, mentions to Graham that "he hated the whole world."[50] The memory of his evil will indeed live on in Charlie's nightmares. It is uncertain for how long.

Ultimately, order is maintained in the film. Although a great spiritual battle has been waged within the American community of Santa Rosa and the personal lives of some of the Newton family, the orderly nature of the cosmos has been recognized. Time marches on—as do the troops overseas—and evil will be vanquished, albeit temporarily, the film seems to imply. This is an unmistakably ambivalent final tone, but one that has been familiar to adherents of this cosmological presumption for centuries. This worldview, far from withering vis-à-vis a direct crisis, faced a resurgence in the 1940s that was reinvigorated by the war—a war that ultimately brought death and mutilation to tens of millions of human lives worldwide. The complex relationship between such a worldview that associates cosmic time with such a temporal military conflict resonates in our global conflicts throughout the world—and will quite probably continue to do so.

---

50. Hitchcock, *Shadow of a Doubt*, 1:47:18.

CHAPTER THREE

The Stranger (1946)

The world, particularly the European world, in 1946 was in shambles. Civilization had not experienced such abrupt, wide-scale annihilation since the Black Plague. It had been a hemoclysm. Some aspects of American culture projected the optimism of unlimited possibilities for the newly liberated world in the future. But the years immediately following WWII also included artifacts of great angst, loathing, and dire introspection. These years produced critically acclaimed, commercially successful films dealing with a host of devastating psychological, social, physical, economic, religious, and criminal problems. Films such as *The Long Weekend* (1945), *Mildred Pierce* (1945), *The Best Years of Our Lives* (1946), *Gentlemen's Agreement* (1947), *The Snake Pit* (1948), *Pinky* (1949), and *The Set-Up* (1949).

Although local celebrations throughout America on V-E Day and V-J Day unmistakably announced an unprecedented collective sense of relief, the immediate postwar period was more generally filled with signposts of anxiety concerning the present or future. "With the fading of the linear vision of progress, Americans yielded to the darker imagery and flashbacks of film noir . . . and, finally, to a deep sense of cultural stasis. Desperate for a more comforting perspective on the present, many Americans sought refuge in frontier myths and bucolic reveries."[1]

In the wake of war, order had been reestablished. And if God created the cosmos as a fundamentally orderly system, the war had paradoxically preserved it. Instead of the *chaoskampf* that guided Wehrmacht ideologues to a destructive catharsis, the Allied championship of just war theory, multilateral coalition, cooperative democracy, stewardship, and meritocracy demonstrated the fundamental orderliness of God's cosmos by anointing America as the latest exceptionalist avatar.

Generally speaking, the cosmological presumption survived, though severely challenged by the complex and disturbing questions framing the war. Survivors, victims, and even perpetrators often look to an historical narrative to gain insight or wisdom. By commiserating about past tragedies, for example, one may derive the resolve to move forward through life—to make emotional progress, as it were. Looked at in this way, time and timekeeping devices served the postwar period as a clearly identifiable emblem of the orderliness of the cosmos. The suspense of temporality, typified by the "interruption" of global war, was over. A new suspenseful scenario had just begun.

FOR HIM THE BELL TOLLS

Just weeks after Congress authorized an initial $7 billion lend-lease package for the Allied war effort, Orson Welles's first feature film, *Citizen Kane* (1941), premiered on Broadway. After much controversy, the now most canonical American film was first seen by movie audiences on May 1, 1941. The famous opening of the film boasted an artifice patterned after the newsreel series *The March of Time*, called *News on the March* in the film. Welles himself, perhaps the most famous voice actor on the radio at the time (especially after his notorious 1938 *War of the Worlds* Halloween broadcast), actually voiced some of the narration for some *The March of Time* films. The series represented his radio debut in 1935 and actually provided Welles

---

1. Graebner, *Age of Doubt*, 68.

with his first regular radio employment.[2] The hearty attitude of a return to progress after the discontinuity of wartime voiced by the clichéd, portentous announcer helped fuel, among other things, the baby boom generation. Originally designed to support readership of newly formed *Time* magazine, the series quickly became one of the most popular means to global news, due in part to its delivery directly into the movie theater programming.

The audio-visual allusion to *The March of Time* in the opening reel of *Citizen Kane* was unmistakable to its original audiences. Both the series and the reference specifically use time terminology—which always serves as a symbol for order. The allusion also reappropriates the emplotment used by the newsreel series. That is, the newsreel contextualized global conflict as a continuing story. It offers the news as an unfolding of characters, events, and themes that were easily accessible to moviegoing audiences in the pre-digital age. The emplotment technique, so fundamental to narrative history and current events, offers a simple way to orient the contemporary crisis as part of an orderly narrative that will ebb and flow in its action. Yes, tragedies will occur in the war, it suggests, but so will victories that confirm the orderliness of the cosmos. This narrative orientation, so central to *The March of Time*, is cleverly borrowed to orient the viewer to the *roman à clef* of *Citizen Kane*. It will be shown that although Welles's worldview may have been personally ambiguous, conflicted, or vague, an interest in time as a sign of the cosmological presumption runs through his films.

Orson Welles's professional work ethic as a director was antithetical to that of Alfred Hitchcock's. Also raised Catholic, he had quickly abandoned any religious creedal or rote ritual activities, particularly because his Catholic mother died young, his father was an adamant agnostic, and his guardian regularly berated the Bible. Late in life he said, in a characteristically nebulous manner, "In a strange way, I even accept the divinity of Christ. The accumulation of faith creates its own veracity. It does this in a sort of Jungian sense, because it's been made true in a way that's almost as real as life."[3] This ambiguous position towards institutional religion may or may not be discerned in his life and work. What is significant here is his unaffiliated attitude, which one probably cultivates from a lifetime survival strategy based on improvisation, obstinance, and bravado. Given this, he perpetually eluded attempts to pinpoint his precise beliefs, theological or otherwise. He once said, "If you try to probe, I'll lie to you. Seventy-five percent of what I

---

2. Berg and Erskine, *Encyclopedia of Orson Welles*, 249–50.
3. Estrin, *Orson Welles Interviews*, 142.

say in interviews is false."[4] The reams of contradictory research on his life, work, and words seem to bear out this motto.

One of the notorious claims about Welles the director perpetuated in most of the canonical Welles scholarship is his disastrously obsessive multitasking. Notwithstanding his highly sporadic post-*Kane* career, he would almost always be filming two pictures at once, or directing a play while acting in a film, or writing a screenplay while raising funds, and so on. This sort of chaotic approach to work in an industry based heavily on collective revenue from the creation of a complete, marketable, final product led to countless problems. On the one hand, he abruptly became poison with the studio executives, hamstringing his directorial career for the rest of his life. His most fecund and promising films (virtually all of them) suffered from compromised truncations, crucial alterations, and incomplete footage.

His chaotic approach also hampered scholars' efforts to settle on any definitive versions of his works. Some, like *Citizen Kane*, are squarely authorial, due to his unprecedented permission to make the final cut. Others, like *Mr. Arkadin/Confidential Report* (1955; even the title varied from America to Britain), now exist in at least three significantly different versions, despite the Herculean reconstruction efforts of archivists Stephan Drössler and Claude Bertemes for a Criterion DVD release in 2006. Various archival reconstructions have produced salvaged versions based on only partial footage and released in art house theaters, such as *Othello* (filming finished in 1952; reconstructed in 1992) and *It's All True* (filming finished in 1942; reconstructed in 1993). Another feature, *The Other Side of the Wind*, began filming in 1970 and was in suspense for decades due to some convoluted complications involving a French thief and Ayatollah Khomeini of Iran.[5] In a dramatic coda typical of Welles's life and work, *The Other Side of the Wind* was ultimately reconstituted and released in 2018 on Netflix, along with an original companion documentary chronicling the postproduction epic. While the authorship of these works is only one of the primary questions posed by scholars, the question of exactly which versions are definitive poses altogether more confounding challenges. And these are only a few of the problems that have resulted from Welles's personal and professional chaos. Consequently, perhaps more than those of any other A-list director, his films require significant qualification.

Nonetheless, themes related to cosmos and time can be found throughout his corpus. In his first (short) film, apparently a surrealist parody, *The Hearts of Age* (1934), Welles plays a "white-garbed Father Time figure"

4. Callow, *Road to Xanadu*, xi.
5. Rosenbaum, "Battle over Orson Welles."

holding a globe.⁶ This image of a possibly transcendent figure was the very first appearance of Welles in a moving picture and, without investing the project with too much gravity, seems to at least set a cosmic tone for the rest of his film work. In the film, a woman (played by his wife) sits astride a tolling bell, an unmistakable reference to watching time. The discontinuity of time and place represented by the film's editing and expressionistic sets signals the touchstone of surrealist cinema. As surrealists such as Andre Breton argue, film is an oneiric, and therefore absurdist, experience.⁷ The use of the piano especially seems to allude to other short surrealist films such as Luis Buñuel's *An Andalusian Dog* (1928). The associations between the unconscious dream state and the cognitive state of watching a film (although tenuous) have already been identified by early cognitive film scholars. Probably improvising this project, Welles seems to have taught himself how editing can produce a sense of temporal continuity or discontinuity, a lesson any first-time editor learns.

But emblems of time and cosmic order populate his other films as well. In the "Four Men on a Raft" sequence of *It's All True* (1942), the journey of the four heroic fishermen is mediated by their penultimate destination at Tenerife.⁸ As they enter the church for sanctification, the church's façade shows a clock tower (complete with hour and minute hands) on the right of the structure and a cross topping the other tower. The church as an institution serves to represent cosmic time and the intervention of Christ's incarnation into historical time. The four Brazilian heroes enter into the church that uses its very architecture to show time as order. Since no sound was ever recorded for the film, the image is especially poignant, for it is intelligible regardless of language.

Welles's second feature, *The Magnificent Ambersons* (1942), whose current version was dramatically recut before release against his wishes, seems to display a minor meditation on the theme of time, speed, pace, and historical change. These themes are characterized by the early development of the automobile in the film. In an opening scene illustrating the relative slowness of late nineteenth-century travel, Welles the voice-over narrator explains that there was "time for everything."⁹ It is significant that the early development of the automobile coincides historically with the development of film in the late nineteenth century. One of the film's fictional car inventors, Eugene Morgan, says that "when times are gone, they're not gone,

6. Berg and Erskine, *Encyclopedia of Orson Welles*, 143.
7. Breton, *Manifestoes of Surrealism*, 36.
8. Benamou, *It's All True*.
9. Welles, *Magnificent Ambersons*, 0:02:38.

they're dead. There aren't no times but new times."[10] Times are always new, in the lived experience of the moment. Joseph Cotten, who plays Morgan, issues a similar gnomic statement as Uncle Charlie in *Shadow of a Doubt* when he tells his family that "today's the thing." The Amberson house décor shows the grandfather clock on the stairs, a reminder of the passage of time and the cosmic order of the universe. All along, the car is an unmistakable reference to the associations between machines and progress so typical of the modern age. And what is motion but the experience of time and space?

Even in his last feature, *F for Fake* (1973), Welles exploited the representation of time and order. At the outset, his first-person promise directed straight to the audience is: "During the next hour everything you hear from us is really true, based on solid facts."[11] The sleight of hand that Welles executes here hinges on the experience of time. The first hour of *running time* represents a factual documentary paradoxically concerning forgers and fakers, but the film does not end after one hour. It continues. What occurs after that in the film is free from his pledge to be truthful. In fact, the rest of the film is fictional. First-time audiences are usually surprised by his truthful claim to be truthful only up to a certain point in time. Ironically, if the audience takes Welles at his word, they would know exactly *when* they are being lied to. In his last directorial gesture, he leaves the audience contemplating the centrality of time in the film experience.

How can this paradox of a concern for cosmic time in films and personal and professional chaos be reconciled? Perhaps one simple way is to reexamine the inflated claims in support of Welles's authorship. Both those who characterize Welles as the apotheosis of the French New Wave auteur theory (most notably Andre Bazin, Jean-Luc Godard, and François Truffaut) and those personally, intellectually, and artistically invested in him as friends (such as Peter Bogdanovich and Barbara Leaming) tend to accentuate the degree to which Welles's central vision predominates his material. The word "genius" is typically invoked as often as the word "author" or "auteur." While his talents for creativity in film dialogue, composition, and editing are indisputable, overemphasizing the singularity of these films presents an oversimplification at best and obfuscation at worst. The collaboration of production work, particularly in midcentury studio films, necessarily contextualizes any claims pointing to a directorial *Übermensch*. Welles himself references the issue in his self-reflexive *F for Fake* and ponders how the thousands of artists who created one of the world's most remarkable artistic works, Chartres Cathedral, are entirely anonymous.

10. Welles, *Magnificent Ambersons*, 0:16:10–0:16:16.
11. Welles, *F for Fake*, 0:03:00–0:03:05.

Another qualification that should not diminish Welles's creative flair, but should complement it, is the recognition that commercial studio films not only produce a worldview but reflect it as well. This complex relationship helps explain the cultural complicity in the creation of films as artifacts. In other words, films are not simply the manifestation of a particular director, writer, or producer; neither are they the simple actualization of a collective worldview that consumers demand is produced. Films are indeed produced, but the credit (or blame) for their creation should not rest so squarely on a single entity or institution. Film production and reception is a diffused collaboration of values and norms. This position is the one espoused by many scholars of cultural production, historical poetics, and cinema theory, such as David Bordwell, Janet Staiger, and Kristin Thompson, and can be helpful in explaining the role of order in an otherwise chaotic life.

One other perhaps obvious explanation for this apparent interest in cosmic time is the ubiquity of deadlines in the film world. Business-minded executive producers such as the assiduous and imperious Harry Cohn blatantly demanded timeliness from his culture machine. Especially during the age when Hollywood went to war, lateness in business was overlaid by associations with insurrection, hierarchical transgression, and sinfulness. Although befitting a Byronic *artiste* like Welles, a disdain concerning the encroachment of mechanistic time over the artistic process has simply never been good business in the era of modernity. A film's delayed completion often creates financial chaos, causing overtime costs to rise, agitating investor anxiety, and requiring the recalibration of projected figures. Hollywood studios, after all, are Weberian institutions par excellence. Even today, many big-business studio films finished on time that boast marketable stars exist in a netherworld between postproduction and popular release. Once again, Welles's chaotic ethic, combined with various other factors, often created disaster. One of the only films he completed on time and under budget in his whole career was *The Stranger*.[12]

STRANGER IN A STRANGE LAND

During the war years, Orson Welles threw himself into various traditionally themed war-related projects. Of course, for him these typically included elaborating on the virtues of democracy, American culture, and English-language masterpieces. On December 7, 1941, the day that Pearl Harbor was bombed, Welles's live voice reached millions of Americans during a

---

12. Brady, *Citizen Welles*, 380.

radio broadcast titled "Between Americans."[13] From America's entry into the war until the unconditional surrender of Japan on August 15, 1945, he broadcast well over one hundred radio shows. During that period, he wrote numerous articles in magazines such as *Free World*, a periodical whose honorary board included Albert Einstein and Chiang Kai-shek and whose other contributors were prominent writers such as Ernest Hemingway, Thomas Mann, and Archibald MacLeish. Often extolling the virtues of democracy and the urgency of global threat, Welles's writing became a central part of his patriotic expression. He recorded a series of great democratic speeches for Decca records. Under the aegis of the "Good Neighbor" foreign policy, he was appointed by the administration to be a special ambassador to Latin America, charged with generating hemispheric good will. The catalyst for his part in the project was the film *It's All True*, which, though its guidelines were vague, was designed to emphasize America's interest (via Hollywood) in Latin American culture. This venture was certainly not frivolous at a time when several South American governments were already pro-fascist or crypto-fascist. He also worked fervently for Franklin Roosevelt's 1944 reelection campaign, stumping heartily for months. Welles's fervency was driven by, as Simon Callow writes, "an apocalyptic sense of the forthcoming struggle for the world's soul . . . in which the beloved liberal of the world [Roosevelt] must be supported; there could be no more important task."[14] By the end of the three and a half years of war and broadcast, Welles was one of the foremost voices of American identity.

Like several notable Hollywood culturati, Welles did not serve in combat. Branded with a 4-F status due to bronchial asthma, flat feet, and a scoliotic spine, he was rejected by the Armed Forces for active duty. Also, like several of his filmmaking colleagues, he received deferment as an essential worker in an industry essential to the war effort, a point he was to characteristically accentuate. Like Hitchcock, who served in neither of the world wars, there was probably an element of the psychological at work in their investment in the war effort. Both directors (for health reasons as well as artistic ones) worked in the relative safety of the home front while their peers suffered and died thousands of miles from home in hostile territory. In Welles's case, this poignancy may have contributed to his political about-face. As late as the summer of 1941, he seemed to publicly support the isolationist cause. Of course, after 1941, isolationists or pacifists betrayed their kinship to insurrectionists, according to the popular mentality. After 1941, everything changed.

13. Welles and Bogdanovich, *This Is Orson Welles*, 20.
14. Callow, *Hello Americans*, 215.

His public dedication to the war effort notwithstanding, Welles, in private, continued to act like an archetypical *monstre sacré*. A notorious womanizer, Welles had countless sexual liaisons throughout the forties, not to mention several extramarital affairs. Addicted to amphetamines, alcohol, and food, his weight swelled over the duration of the war, further confirming the grounds for his rejection by the Armed Forces.[15] He often flew into rages against his personal, artistic, intellectual, and political rivals and friends. His attacks on Roosevelt's opponents became increasingly acerbic, demonstrating the double-edged sword of having Welles as an ally. Incidentally, in 1946, Welles considered running for a Senate seat in his home state of Wisconsin against a "newcomer," Joseph McCarthy.[16] McCarthy would become the most famous architect of the paranoiac Hollywood blacklisting scandal of the early fifties; his chief counsel, Roy Cohn, later successfully defended Donald Trump against federal charges of housing discrimination.

Additionally, Welles publicly denounced whole media industries and political persuasions, seemingly alienating himself from virtually everyone in America at one point or another. He even threw several pieces of furniture from his sixth-floor hotel room in an angry fit. Despite his dutiful and sincere support for America's war-effort propaganda, Welles very quickly became one of the most notorious celebrities in Hollywood.

By the end of the war, he had burned almost all his bridges. Some, including Welles, would say that those bridges were burned for him. Regardless of the polemics on both sides of this issue, he was unmistakably complicit in his own precarious position in Hollywood. He had been getting by financially by pouring himself into several media-related excursions. He had been writing, acting, and directing sporadically. The "Good Neighbor" film *It's All True* had run aground. He had been fired from RKO and virtually blacklisted from the Hollywood establishment. His marriage to Rita Hayworth had degenerated to its ultimate state. Although still in demand as an actor on the stage, he had been absent from film for a period of fifteen months when he finally acted in a minor film called *Tomorrow Is Forever* (1946). Directed by Irving Pinchel (who previously directed an adaptation of John Steinbeck's wartime novel *The Moon Is Down*), the film portrays a returning veteran whose face has been so altered by the war that his wife no longer recognizes him. He received $100,000 for his part, an amount which quickly evaporated.[17]

---

15. Callow, *Hello Americans*, 188.
16. Gear, *At End of Street*, 127.
17. Heylin, *Despite the System*, 170.

Even after V-J Day, Welles continued to deliver speeches alerting America to the threat of fascism and Nazism. It seemed that the war had turned him into a true believer in the anti-Nazi message he had so emphatically delivered time and time again through the war. As is ostensibly always the case for Welles's biography, he continued to embody a range of contradictions. Although his patriotism seemed as strident as ever, he had been significantly disillusioned by many elements of American culture, especially those related to institutions and their influence. He had acquired a taste of exotic, dramatically different cultures during his duration in Ireland in his teens and in Brazil in his twenties. Welles demonstrated a great affection for Latin American culture. His scintillating relationships with perhaps the most famous Latina actresses in the world, Dolores Del Rio and Rita Hayworth, as well as his focus on Latin America in films and film projects such as *The Lady from Shanghai*, *Touch of Evil*, *It's All True*, *Bonito the Bull*, and *Mexican Melodrama*, all show his Latin-philia in the midcentury period. As with so many other Americans, his thoughts and professional work had so often turned to Europe during the war years, reporting and commenting on the military and later diplomatic events occurring on that continent. Two years after the end of the war, he would dramatically break his umbilical cord with America and live around Europe during a decade-long semi-exile. In 1947, he was cast adrift in the world.

It was right at this crucial juncture that Welles found himself with an acting job for independent film producer Sam Spiegel, whose Academy Award-winning Best Pictures *On the Waterfront* (1954), *The Bridge over the River Kwai* (1957), and *Lawrence of Arabia* (1962) would make him a mogul. Welles must have welcomed the work after a dearth of materialized offers. Spiegel offered Welles the chance to star in a film for a rather modest production company, International Pictures, which would eventually be distributed by RKO. Like several prominent Hollywood producers in the 1940s, Spiegel was both Jewish and an émigré. He had overseen film productions in Berlin until the watershed year of 1933, when Hitler's Nazi regime came to power and commenced his genocidal crusade against people like Spiegel. Spiegel had been forced to leave Europe because of Nazi persecution, and now it was time for Spiegel to retaliate.

The proposed film, tentatively titled *Date with Destiny*, would offer a postwar caveat concerning the lingering but deadly threat posed by the Nazis. It dramatized how the Nazi leader who masterminded the Holocaust eluded capture by posing as a history teacher at a Connecticut prep school and married the daughter of a Supreme Court justice. The story was co-written by Victor Trivas and Decla Dunning. Trivas was another European Jewish émigré who escaped the Nazis; like Spiegel, Trivas also made films in Germany before the war. Originally from Russia, he moved to Germany and wrote and directed *No Man's Land*, or *Hell on Earth* (1931), which was partially destroyed by the Nazis in 1933 for its strongly antiwar position; it was for this decidedly antiwar statement that the film was awarded the League of Nations Peace Prize the year it came out.[18] Incidentally, the communist composer of *No Man's Land*, Hanns Eisler, later went on to write the national anthem for East Germany, lending another strongly anti-Nazi distinction to the work.[19]

Throughout the war years, Hollywood films of course dominated the global market both in terms of revenue and number of films produced. German and Japanese productions continued to make stolid propaganda films, though definitely not as nuanced as during the 1930s. British film production, overshadowed by Hollywood before the war, operated largely as its satellite during the war. French production was severely compromised by occupation and other national film productions around the world suffered similarly. Consequently, the figure of the Nazi in global cinema typically became the figure of the Nazi provided by Hollywood, which had suddenly acquired a new and powerful kind of monocultural status around the world.

After 1941, films depicting Nazis as threats on the battlefield were commonplace in movie theaters around the world. Films began to depict the hidden threats posed by Nazi insurgents or double agents as well. The Nazi spies in Hitchcock's *Saboteur* (1942), John Huston's *Across the Pacific* (1942), Fritz Lang's *Ministry of Fear* (1944), and Frank Tuttle's *The Hour Before the Dawn* (1944) exemplify the treachery and cunning of such formidable enemies. By the end of the war, the Nazis had become the single most preferred (and easily accessible) target of Hollywood films, although this propaganda wavered during the de-Nazification directives of the Allies occupying the former Third Reich. In 1945, Henry Hathaway's semidocumentary, *The House on 92nd Street*, exposed the domestic Nazi threat after the war by using some neorealist techniques such as shooting on location, casting actual participants, and focusing on the immediacy of the contemporary moment. Two other notable films of the immediate postwar period were not necessarily anti-Nazi in ideology but in the use of the standard suspense conventions of agent infiltration. Fritz Lang's *Cloak and Dagger* and Frank Launder's *I See a Dark Stranger*, or *The Adventuress*, were both released in 1946 and extend the caveat concerning postwar Nazi infiltration long after the fighting in Europe ended. Hitchcock's own 1946 classic, *Notorious*, marks a turning point in this subgenre in that it simultaneously

---

18. Goergen, "Viktor Trivas."
19. Berthomé and Thomas, *Orson Welles at Work*, 119.

humanizes the escaped covert Nazis while exposing the destructive tactics used by those who hunt them down.

So it was that the film Sam Spiegel offered Orson Welles to star in had a distinct, albeit evanescent, niche. Despite the carnivalesque celebrations on V-E Day and V-J Day, and the return to normalcy over the next year, American audiences were still drawn to watching films with gravitas, such as ones continuing to deal with the Nazi threat. Perhaps they had been conditioned by newsreels and propaganda films to accept the occasional disturbing, realistic Nazi film interspersed among the musicals, comedies, and variety films that predominated the era. The title of the script Sam Spiegel offered to Orson Welles, *Date with Destiny*, seems to allude to Franklin Roosevelt's 1936 Democratic Convention speech in which he declaims that this generation of Americans "have a rendezvous with destiny."[20] However, the title would eventually transform through its provenance to *The Stranger*, a change that reflects this turn to a more conflicted attitude common in the postwar period. The story was turned into a screenplay by Anthony Veiller, who had just finished writing seven film projects documenting the war, most notably for the essential newsreel series, *Why We Fight*. He had just adapted Hemingway's *The Killers* (1946) directed by Robert Siodmak, a film noir that hinges on time lines; for example, discovering the sequence of events leads to a fateful epiphany that the protagonist is being set up.

It was hoped that John Huston, a friend of Spiegel and Welles who had earned his reputation on his debut (and now canonical) film noir *The Maltese Falcon* (1941), would direct. Since Huston was shooting his location films for the war effort, he was unable to direct *The Stranger*, although he co-developed the script. Welles asked Spiegel if he could have the chance to do so and, because the right elements aligned, Spiegel agreed. In typical Wellesian style, he would both play the lead and direct. However, the budget and lead casting was out of Welles's hands. He was also reined in by one crucial provision in his contract. He was required to complete the film on time or else financially indemnify the studio.[21] Welles agreed and the contract—along with the time line—was made legal. It was a chance for Welles to demonstrate his ability to be professionally disciplined, frugal, and timely, exactly what he had *not* been able to do for years, if ever. It was another quest to represent cosmic order through film.

It is possible that Welles's affectations for Rankin were inspired by the anti-Semitic congressman from Mississippi, John Rankin, who at this time was the main force behind the House Un-American Activities Committee,

---

20. Dallek, *Franklin D. Roosevelt*, 256.
21. Heylin, *Despite the System*, 170.

described as "gaunt, with hollow eyes and generous tufts of gray hair," much like Orson Welles's appearance in the film—minus the moustache; this touch would have added a specific political flair to a story about a secret Nazi in America laboring to undermine Jewish influence.[22] Another European Jew, veteran actor Edward G. Robinson, was cast as Mr. Wilson, the lead government agent hunting the crypto-Nazi. Robinson had recently become a top film star in suspense classics such as Anatole Litvak's *Confessions of a Nazi Spy* (1939), Fritz Lang's *Scarlet Street* (1945), and Billy Wilder's *Double Indemnity* (1944), in which he also plays an investigator. Loretta Young, who also came as part of the contract deal, plays Mary, the Nazi's wife. At the age of thirty-three, Young had already appeared in over eighty films. There were only two actors Welles had directed before: extras Erskine Sanford, a guest at the party without lines, and Gerald Pierce, the uncredited boy who throws paper shreds through the woods. The rest was terra incognita for Welles, although the thematic material concerning the furtive Nazi threat was strikingly familiar. But he had always been drawn to the unknown. His professional career as a director had always been one typified by suspense. Since *Citizen Kane*, his career was suspense personified.

ESTABLISH TIME

The film began shooting in early 1946 on schedule. Welles played the secret Nazi mastermind, Franz Kindler. Kindler's name was cleverly encrypted in the moniker of his new persona, history teacher Charles Rankin: F(RAN)z (KIN)dler. Rankin/Kindler stands as a pillar of society in the small town of idyllic Harper, Connecticut, teaching the sons of many of America's leading families. As the film begins, he is about to be married to Mary Longstreet, daughter of Supreme Court Justice Adam Longstreet. In addition to teaching at the Harper prep school, he is also the unofficial horologist of the church tower, fixing and maintaining the central timekeeping feature of the town. As the film reveals, Rankin is not only a horologist but a horomaniac. This mania serves as a crucial clue that leads Wilson, the agent hunting him, to suspect his true identity. In Germany, Kindler displayed an idiosyncratic passion for clocks. This clue illustrates Schopenhauer's adage that a man can will what he wants but cannot will what he wills. In other words, his secret passion betrays him because it is indivisibly intrinsic to his identity. Wilson even says of Mary's marriage to Rankin, "People can't help who they fall in love with." This essentialist premise would play a crucial role in tracking down escaped

---

22. Gabler, *Empire of Their Own*, 355.

murderous monomaniacs in later films as different as *Marathon Man* (1976), *Silence of the Lambs* (1991), and *The Secret in Their Eyes* (2009).

Unlike the antagonists in those films, the fact that Rankin's monomania is for clocks and timekeeping devices is of supreme importance for this study. The film never explains how a German clock was to surmount the colonial-style church building. But such a striking indicator seems to reference several thematic elements at once. It immediately alludes to the distinct tradition of polyvalence between religious, state, and scientific authorities appropriating the regulatory device of the town clock. The same ostensibly innocuous device that regulates behavior in Santa Rosa and all over the industrialized world is regulating behavior in this town as well. The German influence in colonial America is also referenced by the clock. We are reminded that Rankin was by no means the first German to inhabit America, Connecticut, or perhaps even Harper. The German influence in the American colonies and republic has been unquestionable. Nonetheless, xenophobia has sporadically targeted Germans and German-Americans, most notably during the two world wars when even German culture groups became defunct due to legal restrictions and social pressure. Dwight D. Eisenhower was perhaps the most prominent American exponent of German descent of the entire midcentury period and he became supreme commander of the Allied forces during the war. Despite their many contributions, Germans in America have, from time to time, been treated as strangers.[23]

In both of the wars during which Americans fought against Germans, ethnic animus was also recruited for the war effort. But on a greater level, racism has often been appropriated by patriotism in global conflicts. Etienne Balibar goes so far as to claim that racism is always intrinsic to nationalism. In his words, "racism is not an 'expression' of nationalism . . . but a supplement internal to nationalism, always in excess of it, but always indispensable to its constitution." He asserts that "it cannot be by chance that the genocide of the Indians became systematic immediately after the United States . . . achieved independence."[24] The nation's ethnic basis for Anglo-centric criticism of German-Americans (especially during wartime) is a highly problematic construction, although during wartime the illogic of such premises are often elided in public discourse. For proponents of the "deep nation," the question is whether or not one regards German ancestry or culture as quintessentially American. It is a question that can have one answer during peace and another during war. It is, of course, framed by creative historicism as well. A skillful manipulation of historical facts can

---

23. Kazal, *Becoming Old Stock*, 171.
24. Balibar and Wallerstein, "Racism and Nationalism," 54.

produce antipathy towards a group of people traditionally considered as intrinsically "American" as those of British or German ancestry. And what is history but an assemblage of "facts" contextualized in time?

Coincidental with the formation of the American republic, another conflict over cosmology tempered much of the ideological turmoil of the French Revolution. Clocks and calendars as emblems occupied a significant part of the radical phase of the French Revolution. In truly modern fashion, many revolutionary intellectuals recognized the importance of waging a cultural propaganda attack against superstition, mysticism, and folk beliefs. Instead of the idiosyncratic, quasi-religious, hodge-podge calendar, consisting of biblically mandated seven-day weeks and months varying in length from twenty-eight to thirty-one days, the Thermadorian calendar offered a rational ten-day week, with twelve months of equal thirty days each. Instead of the equally idiosyncratic twelve-hour clock, consisting of sixty minutes each, the Thermadorian clock offered ten hours per day, each hour consisting of one hundred minutes. Whether this was too much reason for the general populace or the associations with a bloody and sometimes psychotic regime were too difficult to overcome, the Thermadorian chronometry was quickly replaced by the *status quo ante*.[25]

The cousin conflict of the American War of Independence never used these extreme measures but used time in significant ways nonetheless. Perhaps this is due to the fact that Paris in the 1790s was one of the world's epicenters for radical technology and politics, whereas the colonies were unevenly distributed and heterogeneous in many insurmountable ways. For whatever reason, clocks never seemed to play as crucial a role in American Revolutionary propaganda. Perhaps the most famous tower in the textbook version of the American Revolution was not a clock tower at all, but one signaling the arrival of the imperial forces in Boston in 1775; this same tower's signal instigated Paul Revere's famous ride. Hunting Franz Kindler, Mr. Wilson comes to Harper under the guise of an antiques dealer interested in Paul Revere silver. Both time (e.g., history) and patriotism (e.g., Revere) are evoked by this material artifact. He is looking for this artifact—that is, he is interested in watching the passage of time embodied by this object.

One of the most significant challenges in the postrevolutionary period was to establish a new order. In other words, what forces could possibly ease the transition to a status quo once the radical insurgency that instigated the revolution had accomplished its goals? Of course, the most imminent challenges in creating this new order were establishing financial stability and reinforcing national security. It is no surprise that achieving both hinged

25. Aveni, *Empires in Time*, 144–45.

on the popular belief in the new republic's authority and legitimacy. In order to raise taxes or secure foreign loans, people had to trust in America's prospects. In order to conscript troops or build foreign alliances, people had to look positively on America's chances for survival. The establishment of this new order was accomplished by that touchstone of the modern state: citizenship. Citizens that were most able to control their desires, channel their resources, and participate in community events commensurate with the established laws and norms were the best contributors to the new republic. The best symbol of this regulated behavior is the clock. Pointing to this, many new clock towers were built throughout New England during the late eighteenth and early nineteenth centuries.

Like Santa Rosa, Harper is as an archetypical small town, a microcosm of cosmic order, with all its elements in the proper place, operating in a fundamental harmony with all the other elements. The production design of the town, which includes the general store, the school, and the church, was headed by *Kane* veteran Perry Ferguson, who two years later served as

Alfred Hitchcock's art director for *Rope*, which also presented a tight, microcosmic mise-en-scène.[26] Superficially, Harper looks entirely unmolested by the war. Its idyllic nature is mediated by the film's introduction of this community by a postcard in Meinike's hand. A dissolve from the still postcard to a matching shot of the "real" Harper in motion initially shows the bustle of small-town enterprise. People purposefully walk downtown and vehicles move about in an orderly fashion. It is an active, lively town that is quintessentially normal. Besides the cinematic gimmick of animating the postcard (its aspect ratio roughly equals that of a contemporary standard feature film), the postcard signals the new mobility of tourist culture that burgeoned during the postwar boom. Where travel in Hitchcock's cinematic world consists largely of trains, in *The Stranger*, the bus is the primary means of conveyance. It introduces Kindler's comrade, Konrad Meinike, and Wilson into Harper. The bus, which typically runs according to a strict time schedule, helps both these agents of a horrendous global conflict infiltrate this peaceful community order. Mary wonders aloud that if the clock gets fixed, the whole character of the town might undergo a change, noting that the town's character is presently not really very different from the Harper of the eighteenth century."[27]

When he decides to kill his wife because she represents a threat to his cover, Rankin establishes his own time line. In the general store's phone booth, he sketches "establish time" on scrap paper, followed by the precise time line (down to the minute) for Mary's death and his alibi. During the Holocaust, he has learned how to use efficiency to kill effectively. Once again, time is of central importance in creating order, even if that order is murderous. Rankin's chronological precision displays a premeditation that is at once cold and calculating. His horomania also anticipates the time line that authorities will presumably use to investigate Mary's death. To add to this deadly chronological efficiency, he establishes his alibi at Potter's general store, in full sight of the clock tower where he expects his wife will die. By watching the time, literally, his plan anticipates that his orderly life will be recreated through the death of another.

FRONTIER JUSTICE

Just three days after United States forces dropped an atomic bomb on Hiroshima, Japan, the earliest shooting script of *The Stranger* was completed.[28]

26. Gear, *At End of Street*, 139.
27. Welles, *Stranger*, 0:28:10–0:28:14.
28. Heylin, *Despite the System*, 174.

Approximately seventy thousand Japanese people died in the time it takes to watch the opening credits of a film. For the last six months of the war, as many as five hundred thousand Japanese died as a result of US bombing. In one night alone, Tokyo was firebombed, causing the deaths of at least one hundred thousand people in one horrific night. American air raids had firebombed sixty-six cities and destroyed 2.5 million homes, leaving over nine million homeless.[29] One final, devastating atomic bomb instantly killed tens of thousands more Japanese people in Nagasaki the day the script was finished on August 9, 1945.[30] One day before *The Stranger* would open on July 2, 1946, a picture of Orson Welles's wife, Rita Hayworth, adorned the world's next atomic bomb to be detonated after Nagasaki as it descended over its test site.[31]

While the film was being shot, the Nuremberg trials against Nazi officials occurred. Commencing on October 18, 1945, the International Military Tribunal opened its proceedings against twenty-four surviving Nazi leaders on charges of violating international laws. Several subsequent trials occurred throughout the midcentury period. Many members of the Nazi party in fact engaged in unprecedented acts of aggression against civilians and prisoners of war.[32] Specific charges point to the inhumane conditions of the concentration camps, including medical testing, exposure, and torture. The legal grounds for such international standards had always been tenuous, partially due to the fact that they had yet to be tested under such extreme circumstances. The blurring of moral outrage with legal transgression under the guise of international criminal courts struck some minority voices as dubious. United States Supreme Court Justice William O. Douglas famously criticized the IMT trials since "the crime for which the Nazis were tried had never been formalized as a crime with the definiteness required by our legal standards, nor outlawed with a death penalty by the international community. By our standards that crime arose under an ex post facto law."[33] But in 1945, few Americans felt sympathy towards Nazis.

With the recent creation of the United Nations and the International Court of Justice, the world in 1946 confronted the very frontiers of international justice. On what common juridical grounds can such bodies derive the necessary authority and legitimacy that such times demand? This question, and many others, has threatened the sovereignty of such institutions

---

29. Grayling, *Among the Dead*, 72.
30. Ham, *Hiroshima Nagasaki*, 267.
31. Delgado, "Chapter Two."
32. Megargee, "War of Annihilation."
33. Kennedy, *Profiles in Courage*, 198.

ever since. Without legal precedents in case law (national or international) for such bizarre atrocities or crimes against humanity, positive law has always had to be inventive, relying on extrapolation. As demonstrated by the Supreme Court's 1943 decision in the Hirabayashi case that upheld the federal right to incarcerate untried racial groups in concentration camps, interpreting law during wartime is sometimes a creative act. Justice Frank Murphy wrote the critical dissent from this majority opinion. But it is equally possible that William O. Douglas or Hugo Black were in fact the models for *The Stranger*'s Adam Longstreet, the United States Supreme Justice and Charles Rankin's father-in-law. Rankin relishes how being married to the daughter of such an influential figure in the highest level of American government perfectly camouflages his true identity. The justice is "a famous liberal,"[34] he declaims.

Signaling America's official involvement in the rectification of juridical institutions in war-torn Germany is agent Wilson's name. Perhaps the most famous Wilson at the time was Nobel Peace Prize-winning President Woodrow Wilson. President Wilson's legacy has come to connote several interrelated American foreign policy themes: internationalism (e.g., the League of Nations), engagement (American involvement in WWI), peace negotiations (Versailles Treaty) and the spread of democracy (creation of the Weimar Republic and the Wilson Doctrine). Additionally, Wilson's apologetics for white racism as a means to sustain a white power deep nation, most famously seen in his endorsement of D. W. Griffith's *Birth of a Nation* (1915), are attached to the twenty-eighth president's name.[35] For good or ill, this constellation of connotations colors agent Wilson in the film. The first scene of the film positions his identity vis-à-vis the international community. His are the first English lines (of the final edit of the film) heard emanating from the room of internationals, one of which is clearly speaking in French (*"exactement,"* he says). While Agent Wilson represents the Allied War Crimes Commission, an institution created at the true frontier of international justice, he also seems to represent American interests, with his unmistakable Americanisms, knowledge of the law, and phone calls to Washington.

Again, cosmic order is strongly associated with time. At the immediate conclusion of WWII, international law found itself at a relatively new frontier of jurisprudence, trying to define and retroactively prosecute, almost in real time, such concepts as genocide, crimes against humanity, and communal culpability. At the same time, in small-town Harper, Connecticut, citizens maintain law and order. No policemen appear in Harper. Perhaps

---

34. Welles, *Stranger*, 0:13:28.
35. McEwan, *Birth of a Nation*, 80–81.

it is believed that there is no need for them. Crossing the street towards the clock tower, Meinike is almost hit by a car. Like Charlie's desperate journey to the library in *Shadow of a Doubt*, Meinike's haste nearly causes his death. As it is, Meinike's inopportune timing unleashes chaos. He waits with Mary, compromising her life when Rankin discovers that she has met him. He meets Rankin in the middle of a paper chase in the woods. "Join us later. We'll be up 'til dark,"[36] the boys tell Rankin. Due to the awkward timing of their reunion, Meinike is strangled to death by Rankin, believing he has killed the last artifact of his hidden past that can incriminate him in the ongoing war crimes trials.

Wilson's time line is one of his most effective tactics in hunting the Nazi leader. Reconstructing past events lost in time, Wilson enlists Noah to help discover exactly when and where Rankin was on his wedding day. Of course, there is a Hitchcockian irony here that individuals observing propriety and decorum should not inquire too closely into the details of the bedroom. Nonetheless, it is history that assists Wilson in his Nazi-hunting—that and his copious knowledge of clocks. Sporting Wallace Nutting's 1924 classic *The Clock Book*, he uses his mastery of chronometry to identify Rankin as Kindler. He suspects that the clock in the church tower is a late

---

36. Welles, *Stranger*, 0:12:20.

sixteenth-century Habrecht of Strasbourg, the kind with which Kindler would be familiar. Strasbourg, incidentally, approximately translates from German as "crossroads." He examines his suspect list in the hotel room, which he has titled "Arrivals in Harper Last 12 Months," an unmistakable reference to the recruitment of time in service of detective work. While he does so, he looks up and sees the clock tower through his window. The hands of the clock move in reverse. He then casts a discerning expression, as if he now has his prime suspect—the one person in Harper passionate enough to spend the hard labor required to fix such an imposing chronometer.

This incident is pregnant with symbolism. Time turned backwards leads one to the truth. Such methodology is exhibited in the professions of both men: history teaching and detective work. The counterclockwise movement also reminds one that the conventions of mechanistic time can be manipulated. Mary displays the ambivalence (perhaps felt by other citizens) that she likes Harper "the way it is, even with a broken clock."[37] After the clock is fixed, Potter expresses some concern that the clock's tolling will now keep people up. We know that mechanistic time (the same kind that regulated wartime military campaigns and the trains bringing victims to the death camps) has just invaded Harper after a long absence. Also, a loud clock will make Harper a loud place, further incorporating them into the larger, industrialized world.

Whereas the emblems of time in *Shadow of a Doubt* are often ubiquitous but implicit, in *The Stranger* they are ubiquitous but much more explicit. Associations between time and order abound in the film. The film itself exhibits a degree of horomania. For example, it is the discussion of an item in the *London Times* that exposes Rankin's damning assertion that Marx was not a German because he was a Jew—a belief that convinces Wilson that Rankin is indeed a Nazi. Interestingly, at the time, there was a decidedly Communist-friendly leaning in the *Times*, whose assistant editor, E. H. Carr, wrote editorials with a strongly pro-Soviet perspective. Perhaps the most notorious Communist spy in British intelligence history, Kim Philby (who would much later be exposed as a high-ranking mole), also wrote for the *Times* only a few years before.[38] A crypto-Nazi like Rankin likely would have smelled the crypto-Soviet scent of the *London Times*.

After Rankin fixes the clock, the transition between several scenes in the last act is accomplished by a single close-up shot of the clockface. During each of these transition shots, the clock shows the time while the bell tolls. Since these transition shots typically last only a few short seconds and

37. Welles, *Stranger*, 0:28:12.
38. Beloff, "Dangers of Prophecy," 9.

seem to occur at night when the number of tolls is high (11:00 instead of, say, 2:00), it is impossible to tell if the clock is actually tolling the correct time. We may assume so because of the one exception. In the final close-up transition scene, the clock shows 11:00. The transition prefaces the final scene. The next shot focuses on Mary silently waking up in the half dark, with the bell tolling cumulatively over the soundtrack. The musical scoring by Bronislau Kaper (also a European émigré who fled the Nazis) begins, but the tolling continues and is mixed in with it as Mary rises from her bed and goes to the clock tower as if in a dreamlike state. The number of tolls is allowed to finish, confirming the synchronicity of the clock and bell. Mechanistic time seems to have summoned Mary from unconsciousness.

Further playing on the theme of frontier justice, Rankin murders Meinike and kills his dog in the forest. The forest, as in popular American myth and fiction, has often stood as the spatial if not symbolic frontier of civilization. The contemporary film (and novel) *The Ox-Bow Incident* (1943) dramatizes the kind of "frontier justice" or extralegal lynching that unfortunately recurred sporadically throughout American history. Of course, the practice of lynching as "frontier justice" connotes the nefarious heritage of racial violence and white supremacy in America, which not only existed away from view but derived much of its threatening power by the fact that, in some communities, lynching was all but endorsed by its pageantry in public spaces. Notwithstanding, vigilantism is most often empowered on the fringes of civilization—in the forest or frontier for example. As Mary and Wilson confront Rankin in the bell tower, it is clear that Rankin's time is finished. He looks down at the groups of Harper citizens that have been summoned in part by the sounds of the disorderly clock tolling. The power of the community's solidarity is demonstrated by two extreme, high-angle shots from Rankin's point of view. Evoking the popular storming of the cathedral in *The Hunchback of Notre Dame* (1939), which used the same extreme, high-angle shot, Rankin is the analogue of that eponymous marginalized character. Wilson has the captain of the Connecticut state police called, and soon state, federal, or international courts will exert their authority to try his case. Before that happens, however, Rankin is shot, is stabbed by an angel statue circumnavigating the clock, and falls to his death. Frontier justice (and perhaps divine justice) has finally been executed.

Two major suspenseful threats leading to this conclusion had already been introduced earlier in the film. The armed angel automaton had been shown in the clock close-up shots that predominate the scene transitions in the last half hour of the film. Always moving steadily and mechanistically from the "sinister" left side of the frame to the symbolically superlative right side of the frame, the crusading angel automaton wielding an outstretched sword chases the demon around the clockface in a pageant that demonstrates the type of cosmological pageant that resonated throughout Western history, from the Crusades to WWII. It hardly needs pointing out that the pageant is intrinsically chronometrical and horological. But while the avenging angel clearly symbolizes divine justice, it symbolizes the machine as well. In the modern era in which scientific views are popularly received, an orderly creation is a mechanistic creation governed by knowable, fundamental, and impersonal laws and patterns. Potter wonders aloud if it is a "man or woman angel"[39] and then concludes that sex probably does not matter to angels. Agents of the divine, like divine or natural law, operate impersonally and irrespective of human agency. This curious reference to angelic androgyny at once associates the supernatural with creation and the divine with sex.

The other major threat introduced at an early stage of the film is the danger of height. Erroneously boasted as the tallest movie set at the time, the clock tower still eclipsed 120 feet in height.[40] It is known that Rankin works high in the tower, sometimes alone and at night. The potential energy created by a suspended body is a common motif in suspense films. In this case, it is important to remember that the suspense is both cosmological and chronological in nature. The higher the antagonist ascends, this seems to say, the greater

39. Welles, *Stranger*, 0:51:15.
40. Heylin, *Despite the System*, 181.

the danger. Perhaps the most iconic example of this convention appears in the climax of Hitchcock's *Saboteur* (1942), where the Nazi *agent provocateur* hangs precariously from the Statue of Liberty's torch before falling to his death. Like Chekhov's axiom about dramatic suspense that one should never introduce a gun in a story unless it will eventually be fired, one should never send an antagonist up a clock tower unless he will eventually fall. Audiences expect that this should occur, thus implicating them in the conventional unfolding of the suspense. Wilson's fall down the stairs in his rush to capture Kindler and save Mary offers a counterpoint to the fatal fall that will soon occur to Rankin/Kindler. Wilson falls as the clock's bells still echo.

Both the dangers of falling and being impaled by an agent of divine justice culminate with the death of Rankin/Kindler. The termination of Kindler serves as an ultimate act of justice, affirming God's covenant to punish the wicked and reward the righteous. As with the Nazi officials who had already been executed by the time the film was released in May of 1946, and would continue to be executed in the ongoing Nuremberg trials, Kindler's death offers victims and survivors some assurance of finality. Rankin's termination, however, marks an end to small-town America's naïve complicity in the acceptance of the artificial personae of crypto-Nazis. As Welles warned in several radio addresses, Americans would need to be wary of another rise of Nazism in the future. The renegade federal witch-hunts spearheaded by Senator McCarthy and the expansion of the FBI's investigative jurisdiction and techniques over the next few years seemed to point to an institutional pseudo totalitarian rise. Some escaped Nazi leaders (most notoriously Klaus Barbie, Adolph Eichmann, and Josef Mengele) were able to elude capture for decades due to the kinds of false identities Rankin used. Rankin's death occurs on "V-Day in Harper," as Wilson says to the town, yet another reference to time and the restoration of cosmic order.

HOLY FAMILY

Rankin's actual fall echoes the metaphorical fall of humankind. Perhaps the worst modern catastrophe of human devastation had occurred over the previous five years, dramatically underscoring the human proclivity for dehumanizing violence aimed against strangers. The fall of humankind in the Genesis account of the Hebrew Torah and Christian Old Testament, often termed "lapsarian," has to some degree produced a theology that involves the cosmological presumption that it is divine justice that orders the human world. In order words, Adam and Eve, the first man and woman, sinned against God and were eternally banned from paradise unless an agent of God's justice—a redeemer—intervened at some time in human history. Known as original sin, the presumption that humankind perennially suffers as a result of Adam and Eve's decision to sin is a foundation of Judeo-Christian theology. It also sets up all of creation as a cosmic arc of history, from the fall of mankind to the apocalypse, in terms of suspense.

The Supreme Court justice is the patriarchal figure of the film. His name, Adam, thus directly connects the highest juridical authority of the state with a postlapsarian cosmology. It carries a host of connotations, most of them biblical: God's first man, a corruptible creature, a complicit husband, and a sinful patriarch. The biblical patriarchy is further abbreviated by the name of Justice Longstreet's son, Noah. It is Noah Longstreet who is first recruited by the authorities to save his sister. Like Noah in the Judeo-Christian Scriptures, Noah in the film is one of Adam's descendants and saves his family by God's grace. Mary's name also suggests strong scriptural, theological, and ecclesiastical overtones. She is also descended from Adam. She is the virgin who will eventually allow the salvific actualization of the world to be born. While *The Stranger* does not satisfy the requirements of an allegory, it implies these archetypical religious figures. When accentuated, the parochial trope of the holy family helps the film transcend the generic localism of an otherwise standard suspense story. But the holy family also highlights the sacred importance with which the traditional family was imbued during wartime. As historian Claudia Koontz observes, "While Nazi rhetoric evoked the nostalgic myth of a sheltering family, state policy promoted a submissive family that delivered up its members to the total state."[41] Nazi policy offered financial incentives for large, robust families that would serve their communities. American families were treated in roughly similar ways. The family's sanctity was appropriated by the state during the war and used to serve this higher power during its global, geopolitical struggle and beyond.

The wedding and marriage of Mary Longstreet and Charles Rankin centers the film. This consecrated relationship is the first public "event" introduced in the film. According to modern conventions popular during the midcentury period, the core of any family was the marriage relationship. But the roots of this prioritization of marriage go back to the medieval period. By the twelfth century, marriage standards and conjugality had already been largely institutionalized by Western Christianity. Long since having adopted Augustinian theology, the Roman Catholic Church further articulated the severity of sexual sin, especially outside of marriage. Marriage was sacralized and therefore appropriated by the institution of the church.[42] During the modern period, marriage was later conceptualized under state jurisdiction as well, highlighting its polyvalence and its tenacity as a meaningful social expression in constructing the family.

The wedding of Rankin and Mary concretizes his infiltration into this important family of American government. Before the wedding, he is an imposter. After the wedding, he will be recognized by both the state and the church as a full member of one of America's most influential families. Uncle Charlie's threat to the Newtons presages how intimate the infiltration of evil into the family was in the 1940s. The notion of family honor and shame, now representing the residue of a seemingly more naïve era, strongly mediated the ticklish plight of a family that discovers that one of its members is considered a deviant. The threat to the holy family set against a geopolitical backdrop of infiltration found its perhaps most suspenseful filmic expression in *The Manchurian Candidate* (1963), which portrays a

---

41. Koontz, *Mothers in the Fatherland*, 388.
42. Ruether, *Christianity and the Making*, 54.

presidential candidate whose family have been following the global agenda of foreign Communist authorities. Technically, before marriage to an American citizen, Rankin is an alien. After marriage, he is a citizen. Marriage serves here not so much as a religious sacrament (although it is that), but as a quasi-sacrament bestowed by the government in that it transforms a foreign citizen into an American one. It is the closest to a miracle that a federal government can get.

Rankin's liminal state raises a pertinent question concerning his status in the community. At a time when so many men returned to their homes in small towns like Harper all over the country, what did Rankin tell people he did during the war? In what capacity did he serve his country? No doubt he offered a fabricated story believable enough to allow Mary's father to give his consent to the marriage. Since, of course, he served *against* American troops (not to mention the fact that he masterminded the "Final Solution"), he would be considered persona non grata by American audiences in 1946. But he would also be detested for competing against returning veterans for work and status as well. Stealing a plum teaching job, for example, would add insult to injury. A Nazi stealing a potential wife may have been even more anathema. With millions of war veterans attempting to return to normalcy, job-stealing and wife-stealing would have been all the more detestable. This collective negativity, often termed the "postwar crisis of masculinity," was exacerbated by the increased mobility of even more groups of "strangers" worldwide and at home, such as refugees, displaced persons, exiles, émigrés, and migrants.[43]

The pivotal wedding at the outset of the film is contextualized in terms of time and order. It occurs promptly at 6:00, apparently in the church with the clock tower. Their honeymoon commences on a Thursday but must end before the next Friday, when Rankin issues the final examinations to his students. Wilson determines that Rankin murdered Meinike just before his own wedding by collecting the facts and constructing a time line. In the original script, Mary was to meet Meinike while at Mass in the church. Being a devout Catholic, actress Loretta Young objected, saying that her character would not allow such a meeting to distract her from taking the holy Eucharist on her wedding day. The scene was cut and never shot, but this editing adds another religious dimension to the film as well.[44]

We cannot assume that Rankin and his new wife consummate their marriage. However, we do know that for the entire duration of their marriage as it is presented by the film their intimacy is cursed by stress. In fact,

---

43. Cohan, *Masked Men*, 42.
44. Berg and Erskine, *Encyclopedia of Orson Welles*, 433.

one is hard pressed to find any details that suggest they have indeed had sex, even by conventional cinematic signals of the late 1940s. But several details suggest otherwise: hurtful arguments, long periods of separation, and the paucity of endearments or gentle touching in private. Mary is never called by her married name, Mary Rankin, further suggesting a marital disconnection, especially since their marriage relationship centers the film at a time when patriarchal power was being reasserted. Nor can we assume that this stress is caused entirely by suppressing his true identity as a Nazi mastermind of the death camps. The curious motif suggested by the discussion about androgynous angels perhaps offers a clue. A strong analogy between sexual deviancy and spies was promulgated during the midcentury period, a period of great international anxiety concerning issues of identity at home and abroad.

That intimacy problems between Charles and Mary Rankin do not have a purely situational basis (i.e., that Rankin is covering up his notorious past as a Nazi and therefore is emotionally distant from her) opens up the possibility that their estrangement has a deeper sexual cause. I would like to suggest that if the Rankins suffer from intimacy problems, it may be due to the homosexual elements that constitute a subtext of the film. Meinike's dogged quest for Rankin over three continents, the conditions of their illicit meeting in Harper, and their secret exchanges and final embrace in the forest suggest a kind of homosocial bond that parallels the plight of homosexual men living in small-town America in the midcentury period. After all, Meinike came to Rankin on a mission "in the name of . . . the All Highest . . . I mean God."[45] Heylin calls the compromising incident between the two men in the forest Rankin's "guilty secret."[46] Meinike urges Rankin to pray to God for repentance, a common response for struggling closeted homosexuals in a predominantly Judeo-Christian milieu. While it is true that homosocial relationships pervade the military's structuration of social relations during the war, these were largely endorsed and perpetuated by popular culture and military propaganda alike. But where homosocial camaraderie among combat units was celebrated, homosexual activity was definitely repressed. The fear and panic Rankin seems to exhibit after his intimate and incriminating meeting with Meinike in the woods operates with the same narrative trajectory as a closeted homosexual at the time.

That is not to say that Rankin is indeed an actual homosexual, but that his situation promulgates the loose association between spies and homosexuals common in the postwar popular mentality. The fact that Rankin served as such a privileged leader of the Nazi party seems to expose the fact

---

45. Welles, *Stranger*, 0:14:07–0:14:13.
46. Heylin, *Despite the System*, 184.

that Rankin was probably not an active homosexual since Nazi policies so criminalized and demonized homosexual identities, even to the point of consigning thousands of homosexuals to prison and concentration camps for that very transgressive reason. But these subtextual themes draw attention to the upheaval of sexual and gender identities in the immediate postwar period, with males returning to home, women being dislodged from wartime employment, and homosexuals stigmatized as ever by the politicization of "deviant" sexual identities. The closeted Nazi-gay figure in a popular Hollywood film in the late 1940s was soon replaced by the closeted Communist-gay figure in the early 1950s. As Robert Corber argues from an historical perspective, liberal intellectual arbiters informed the politicization of homosexuals, fixing them as a trope of political infiltration.[47] In other words, during the Red Scare, covert Communist operations in America were conceptualized by analogy with homosexual infiltration. Ideologically speaking, homosexuals, like Communists, felt a psychological victimization or alienation that motivated them to secretly recruit others to their cause of ultimately overthrowing the current exploitative power relations. But Corber deals specifically with the associations between Communism and homosexuality. The threat of closeted Nazism in *The Stranger*'s subtext, though ideologically antithetical to homosexuality, serves to explain Mary's final motivation for killing her own husband.

In a pivotal scene between Charles Rankin and Mary, they tensely discuss her father's mysterious phone call summoning only Mary to his house. As we discover later, her father (with Wilson's assistance) will attempt to convince her of her husband's true identity. As Charles and Mary argue, their grandfather clock separates them in the frame. It stands between them, bisecting the frame into two sides, with Charles on the left and Mary on the preferred right side. This is the clock that he regularly maintains. It also betrays his breakdown as he carelessly grabs the bells, causing a literal cacophony in their already charged conversation. The emblem of time once again mediates the boundary between order and disorder.

After the authoritative Wilson and the patriarchal Adam intervene by showing Mary some of the horrifying concentration camp footage (which was still shocking audiences a year after the war's end), Adam appeals directly to Mary as an authority on the law. The authentic footage inserted into *The Stranger*'s diegesis creates a film-within-a-film. In effect the "real" film-within-a-film (microcosm) refers to the "real" horror in the world (macrocosm). In point of fact, the Nuremberg trials mark the first time that graphic film of atrocities was used in a trial as proof of criminal

---

47. Corber, *In the Name.*

wrongdoing.[48] Welles said of his use of the highly evocative archival footage, "I'm against that sort of thing in principle—exploiting real misery, agony, or death for purposes of entertainment. But in that case, I do think that, every time you can get the public to look at any footage of a concentration camp, under any excuse at all, it's a step forward. People just don't want to know those things ever happened."[49] *The Stranger* marked the last time such explicit concentration camp footage was used in a mainstream Hollywood film until *Judgment at Nuremberg* (1961), signaling another profound scotomaphilia. Robert Kolker calls this film's employment of concentration camp footage, brief though it is, "extraordinary," and goes on the suggest that *The Stranger* represents "a provocation of contemporary history for an audience that might have wished to forget what the world had just been through. . . . It examines the acts of forgetting and remembering over the course of time."[50]

Wilson, allied with Adam the patriarch, tells Mary that if Rankin is indeed Franz Kindler, then Mary's marriage is nullified. As spurious as this legal claim is, it at least signals Mary that some moral conditions might actually invalidate a marriage. This is where the homosexual subtext informs the tension caused by the fact that Rankin is an escaped Nazi war criminal. Under what conditions might she be impelled not just to divorce him but attempt to kill him, just days after being married? The endorsement of her marriage annulment argued by her patriarchal Supreme Court justice father, in addition to the horror of being contained in wedlock by a Nazi quasi-homosexual, seems to be enough for this extreme reaction. It seems fitting that their deadly confrontation occurs at the top of the phallic clock tower.

Mary thus serves as the agent of his death. Unlike any traditional female film noir characters typically imbued with the advantages of superior knowledge and duplicitous personae, Mary is the agent that brings about her husband's death with a motivation that is broadcast and rationalized long before the confrontation occurs. Rankin's death, then, is subject to the conditions of autonomous agency. Like Mike O'Hara, the protagonist of *Lady from Shanghai*, Welles's next directorial venture, Mary may be a murderer or an assassin. She may even be acting as an agent of state power, like those millions of Americans given the license to kill other human beings during the war. Is Mary a murderer? Is she an assassin? Has she been given a tacit license to kill by the endorsement of both patriarchal and governmental power? While Rankin's death is definitive (extolled by the clock

---

48. Douglas, "Film as Witness," 324.
49. Welles and Bogdanovich, *This Is Orson Welles*, 189.
50. Kolker, *Extraordinary Image*, 93.

mechanisms whirling wildly out of control), the answers to those questions seem to be frustratingly ambiguous.

KILLING TIME

One of the broader questions that the film introduces is why is this escaped Nazi leader such a horomaniac? This predilection appears to be presented as a fatal flaw since, considering Rankin expresses his worldview through this obsession with clocks and time, it ultimately gives away his true identity. But it may also have served as a conduit for his exceptional organizational talents. In service of the Nazi state, such an obsession with precise timing would have been championed. In the ubiquitous military campaigns during the war, the accurate regulation of men and material by a strict time schedule would have been of prime importance. Regulating the concentration camps with scientific, albeit brutal, efficiency would have been his chief skill set. Of course, the psychological explanation is always possible, and since Wilson attempts at least some psychoanalytical explanations, it is worth noting that the film seems to present the possibility that the psyche operates according to mechanistic rules, not unlike a clock. According to this reductive rationale, if the mind is unhealthily burdened by guilt, fear, or denial, it will inevitably show signs of strain, not unlike a clock that has been left unattended.

But the practical explanation that an effective genocidal mastermind operates according to the dictates of mechanistic time is supported by the ideological explanation as well. One of the scenes cut from the original shooting script involves a speech that Rankin delivers elaborating on the clock's mechanics, which only thinly conceals its symbolic associations with Nazi ideology. Rankin observes:

> The force that runs the clock, the spring or the weight, or whatever it is, is the head of State. The pendulum is his government which transforms his inspirations into law. The train of gears are the working masses . . . formed into economic units which engage each other without friction . . . the teeth are individuals, just as these are of flawless metal, well ground and polished, so must the individual be of good blood, trained and fit physically.[51]

Nazi ideals imagine a cosmic order that structures all meaningful human experiences in service to the state: history, social life, work, war, and death. The propaganda commonly expressed by totalitarian regimes suggests a politically constituted unification of these elements. In other words,

51. Callow, *Hello Americans*, 275.

it is political ideology that connects all of these. Although these ideals found popular support during key fascist regimes in the midcentury period, many inconsistencies and hypocrisies existed in the practical expression of these ideals. Nonetheless, Rankin's choice of metaphor makes the political ideology behind it especially accessible and pedantic because the analog clock in modern society is such a ubiquitous and intrinsic emblem of modernity. For the Nazi, everyone's social location is highly ordered, like all the essential components of a clock. Those pieces that do not fit or are not are perfectly sound are eliminated.

During the dinner conversation between Mary, Wilson, Adam, and the doctor, Rankin reluctantly elaborates on his views of the current state of Germany "as an objective historian," another specialization dealing with the study of time. He advocates a Carthaginian peace for Germany, no doubt a reference to the harsh deinstitutionalization proposals of the punitive Morgenthau plan that would have crippled German industries in the postwar period. The plan originated in 1944 and was made public before the end of the war. Nazi Propaganda Minister Joseph Goebbels even referenced the harsh plan in order to rally Nazi resistance against Allied invasion.

Mary is surprised by his suggestion that Germany should be crushed by the Allies. Rankin reminds us that the world has had little trouble from Carthage in the past two thousand years, a rather blunt, neoconservative perspective. Although Rankin's harsh attitude serves as good intellectual camouflage for a secret Nazi living in America at the time, another ideological reason informs his position. As Hannah Arendt asserts:

> Mass leaders in power have one concern which overrules all utilitarian considerations: to make their predictions come true. The Nazis did not hesitate to use, at the end of the war, the concentrated force of their still intact organization to bring about as complete a destruction of Germany as possible, in order to make true their prediction that the German people would be ruined in case of defeat.[52]

Rankin's belief in the future of Nazi Germany as a phoenix is predicated on his knowledge as an historian. After the end of WWI, the Nazi party rose sporadically and fitfully from popular discontent through democratic channels set up by the Allied victors. The draconian war reparations imposed on Germany in the 1919 Versailles Peace Treaty instigated an economic disaster which was famously and critically predicted by John Maynard Keynes's *The Economic Consequences of the Peace* (1919). The wide-scale discontent and disillusionment following in the wake of Weimar's 1923 hyperinflation,

---

52. Arendt, *Origins of Totalitarianism*, 349.

in tandem with the concomitant scapegoating of Germany's degenerate artistic and intellectual avant-garde, led to the eventual dissolution of the Weimar Republic and the rise of Nazi Party consolidation.

Rankin believes that if the Germans are treated as harshly as they were following the last war, Nazi ideology will ascend again. This positivism demands a faith that the forces of order (as conceived by Nazi ideology) are in perpetual conflict with the forces of degeneracy. Consequently, Rankin can say with great assurance to Meinike that they will "stay hidden until the day when we will strike again."[53] Read in this way, the homicidal and suicidal activities of the last few days of both Hitler's Reich and Rankin's imagined shadow government are rationalized. The *Götterdämmerung* of and by the Third Reich prepared the way for a Fourth. Hitler's final days in his chthonian Berlin bunker presage Rankin's final minutes high in Harper's clock tower, where he could look down on the world like God. As with Hitler in his bunker, Rankin in the clock tower finds himself surrounded, destroyed by the very elements of his passion and profession.

As a legacy, Rankin has indubitably left his intellectual imprint on his students, the privileged young people who will one day presumably lead America (and the world) as adults. The only lesson presented in the film concerns an introduction to "Frederick der Große." The textbook version

53. Welles, *Stranger*, 0:13:45–0:13:53.

of Frederick the Great typically associates this German aristocrat with the *grand homme* theory of history, absolutist rule, and pan-Germanic irredentism. The *grand homme* theory, so ever-present in conventional history textbooks, stresses the achievements of single autonomous agents who act as the prime movers of history. The great men of history accomplished policy goals, built states, and influenced great masses of people. As a result, the study of history is reduced to the biographical study of great men. The traditional canon of these demigods usually included the exclusive requisites of being wealthy, privileged, white males—criteria that resonated in plutocratic Nazi texts on history.

Frederick the Great, like Hitler, was a proponent of absolutist rule. While eighteenth-century absolutism differed greatly from twentieth-century totalitarian rule, the fact that both advocated strong centralization unified by the *l'état, c'est moi* head of state is evoked by Rankin's choice of historical subject. Rankin also introduces King Frederick II by some of his titles, one of which is "Prince of Poland." Frederick famously assisted in the acquisition of Poland in the eighteenth century. As German military prowess steadily deteriorated in the last year of the war, Joseph Goebbels reassured Hitler by citing the historical precedent of Frederick the Great's victory in the Seven Years War despite his prospects appearing hopeless. Goebbels's radio broadcast included Frederick the Great's defiant claim, "We are faced with either death or victory."[54] Frederick's Prussia as an historical prototype of Hitler's Third Reich may be a bit unwieldy as a claim, but nonetheless, enough resonance exists that, if Rankin is a skilled enough ideologue-teacher (though this sounds like a contradiction in terms), he may be able to exploit the connections for propagandistic reasons in future lessons for his impressionable students. The basic irredentist rationale exploited by Frederick's expansionist policies was virtually the same as those used in Hitler's expansionist policies in the late 1930s that successively annexed Sudetenland, Czechoslovakia, Austria, and eventually Poland, the last of which effectively instigated the beginning of WWII.

Two time-related elements charge this brief but significant scene. Rankin checks his private time line for Mary's death, titled "establish time," which he reads covertly as the students prepare for class. Standing in front of the class, he has constructed a series of events that he predicts will result in his wife's death. Exploited knowledge of the past to bring about future destruction therefore recurs here. During this indoctrination scene in the classroom, the Gruen wall clock faces the students, fixed to the wall above their teacher. Framed in this way, with a low-angle shot,

---

54. Longerich, *Goebbels*, 672–73.

the clock outranks the teacher in height. Both authorities (the teacher of historical knowledge and the regulator of mechanistic time) combine their temporal forces for the sake of demonstrating cosmic order for this future generation. The other value of this composition is purely cinematic. By offering both Rankin's face and the clock's face on the same plane, we are able to simultaneously read his affectations while anticipating what tragedy will likely occur. The effect superimposes the quasi-Nazi use of history for indoctrination onto the suspense of temporality. The question "What happened?" collides with the question "What is going to happen?" in the context of filmed suspense.

In a twenty-first-century reception of these two questions, we can ask the same double question of genocide. Since *The Stranger*'s release, genocidal activity has taken the lives of millions of victims, from Cambodia to Rwanda to Bosnia. Yet these experiences exist on a continuum and in geohistorical contexts. Violence of various non-genocidal kinds continues to be perpetuated, and individuals throughout the world are complicit in direct and indirect ways in the extermination of human beings. Although the immediate questions raised by the film are superficially resolved, the broader questions remain. As Jochen Strack suggests, "A complete answer may lead to rationalization; or to the dangerous assumption that what *they* did *then* cannot happen again. Leaving the 'why' question somewhat unanswered may help future generations stay alert."[55]

---

55. Strack, "One German's Response," 22 (emphasis original).

CHAPTER FOUR

Odd Man Out (1947)

Many cultural artifacts produced in the postwar era express a great anxiety about the future and the nature of identity vis-à-vis the old orders. But this generalization must be tempered by the way it is framed. Even in small-town America, angst and alienation counterpoised the rosy images of Technicolor Hollywood films. In Europe, the explicit visual landmarks of violence persisted for years after WWII, exemplified by the obliterated architecture, fractured infrastructure, and mutilated bodies that populated the entire region. But this destruction is animated by harsh, neorealist films such as Roberto Rossellini's *Open City* (1945), *Paisan* (1946), and *Germany Year Zero* (1948). British postwar films generally took a different direction, though. The synthesis of the cosmological presumption with the horrifying and inescapable realities of the recent war years produced cinematically traditional and entertaining (and mildly escapist) narrative films such as 1945's *Brief Encounter, Blithe Spirit,* and *I Know Where I'm Going.*

While still heavily involved in producing explicitly war-related films, the British film industry, like the American, began to produce a greater variety of genre films, partially since the economy supported it. In the late 1940s, Britain produced such widely diverse films as *The Rake's Progress* (1945), *Green for Danger* (1946), and *Against the Wind* (1948), all of which are oriented in relation to the war. Even the new crowd-pleasing Ealing comedies often explicitly refer directly to the devastation of the war, as in the opening scenes of *Passport to Pimlico* (1949) that depict the last undetonated German bomb in metropolitan London, which explodes to reveal an ancient treasure trove buried underneath. The orderly world of these films is colored by assertions of British identity (e.g., the numerous conventional period pieces and English-language classics) as well as real-world difficulties (e.g., the emergence of a Brit noir genre). Questions of identity and imperialism imbue these films and the cosmological presumption with an inflection of postwar realism.

ANOTHER WAY AHEAD

During WWII, numerous American and British filmmakers were considered essential to the war effort. The official rationale for this was that these professional communicators represented a necessary component in the propaganda war, a relatively new facet of modern total war, a premise which by the end of the war had become axiomatic. While many premier celebrities, directors, screenwriters, and cameramen volunteered for active combat duty, several did not. Alfred Hitchcock and Orson Welles were among the most notable film personnel to stay on the home front, working for the government by participating in the propaganda war. Some American directors like John Huston and Frank Capra shot highly praised combat documentaries (*San Pietro* and *Why We Fight*, respectively) as virtual reportage about the course of the war, even to the point of making audiences miserable.[1]

One of the most celebrated contemporary war documentaries was the 1945 Anglo-American coproduction *The True Glory*. Released just months after the end of WWII, the film documents the last year of the European war, from the Normandy invasion to the seizure of Berlin, thus providing a film narrative of these events of recent history. Concluding with an image of an armed soldier striding in front of the two tall but severely compromised church towers, the voice-over narration memorializes the sacrifices of those represented by appealing to that traditional grand narrative of Western history: progress. "What are the spoils [of victory?]" asks the narrator. "A chance to build a free world, better than the one before—maybe a last chance. Now the time has come to put our victory to the test . . ."[2] The finality of this address also opens the possibilities for the future, thus orienting the cinematic experience in a specific chronological moment. As the camera slowly pulls away from a map centered around Berlin, the narrator offers a prayer to God concerning "the true glory." This evocation of the polyvalence of religion and nation, aided by military science and offered for ratification by the pseudo-authority of popular consumers through the medium of film, encapsulated the ongoing progression towards a better world that necessitated such violence. *The True Glory* won an Academy Award for Best Documentary Feature

1. Harris, *Five Came Back*, 395.
2. Reed and Kanin, *True Glory*, 1:22:51–1:23:14.

which was refused by its co-director in memory of those who lost their lives while making the film. That director was Carol Reed.

Reed had started his career as a British stage actor, like his father, Sir Herbert Beerbohm Tree. Tree was one of the most famous stage actors of his time and directed the first movie (clocking in at around four minutes) based on a Shakespeare play, *King John*, in 1899.[3] Carol Reed came under the tutelage of writer (and two-time director) Edgar Wallace, best known to moviegoers now for helping to create the original 1932 *King Kong* screenplay. Unlike his father, Reed then started acting in feature films, starting in 1929. Six years later, he started to direct exclusively, and over the next decade he directed eighteen films in Britain, finishing this run with *The True Glory*. Since Hitchcock and many other notable British directors had emigrated on the eve of WWII, Reed became one of the most successful film directors and certainly in the same league as David Lean, Michael Powell, and Sydney Gilliat. Of course, directors in the British studio system were typically not treated as celebrities, especially during wartime. Hitchcock had been a remarkable exception. Reed's professional comportment therefore meshed well with these conditions. Characteristically reserved in public, he preferred to leave private affairs (of which he had many) entirely private. Even the index of one of his few biographies to date, authored by Nicholas Wapshott, separates Carol Reed (private life) from Carol Reed (professional life).[4]

To many who did not directly work with him, Reed remained a cipher. He rarely granted interviews and questioned the need for them. He maintained an effective organizational compartmentalization over his projects, focusing certain skills on the set and others at home. In his personal reluctance to enter the limelight as a director, he represented the antithesis of both Alfred Hitchcock and Orson Welles. He disliked Hitchcock's cultivation of the director's cult and mistakenly assumed Hitchcock only directed thrillers. A director, in Reed's opinion, should show his skill by demonstrating his versatility over genres and self-immolation to the picture.[5] Welles's flamboyant, albeit ingenious, extra-cinematic antics were certainly not befitting the decorum of a proper British craftsman, he suggested. Indeed, even in this respect he could be classified as a nonauteur. Reed's life seems to demand that we see him as a director of films, and little else should be of concern. Reed's biographer admits the difficulty of unearthing the psychological details that biography readers usually expect: "The process of researching the

---

3. Best, "King John."
4. Wapshott, *Carol Reed*.
5. Wapshott, *Carol Reed*, 229.

life of Carol Reed has, therefore, been like that of a picture restorer, removing years of grime and varnish to reveal a lost masterpiece."[6]

It was not surprising that a man such as Reed would be chosen to direct *The True Glory*. Though he carefully discerned the options available and did a relatively safe stint in the Home Guard, he served geographically much closer to the constant threat of death or dismemberment than his American counterparts, Orson Welles and Alfred Hitchcock. War, like directing a film, is a multifaceted, collaborative, outcome-based experience. Both demand selflessness and bravery. Two films released during Britain's darkest hour in 1940 brought him international attention, *The Stars Look Down* and *Night Train to Munich*. His skill for creative composition, editorial variety, and synthesis of sound and image were soon known by producers in America and Britain looking for the newest reliable talent.

Reed's combat drama *The Way Ahead* premiered three days after the Normandy invasion of June 6, 1944, confirming his ability to direct a realistic war film that effectively engages with the reservations hindering contemporary audiences from fully supporting the war effort. In this sense, *The Way Ahead* satisfied various cinematic and extra-cinematic demands, one of which was supporting official government propaganda. His success with the patriotic documentary *The True Glory* thus represented the combination of several pertinent factors: a worldview that prioritizes compartmentalization, a talent for meaningful collaboration, and the ability to produce effective and creative films quickly and with ease were all recruited by the war effort. The fact that he distinguished himself behind the camera and in the war effort propelled him to a new set of postwar possibilities.

But Reed, like his compatriots, also faced the anxieties of a new world order. In this postwar world, boundaries were even more uncertain than in the *status quo ante*, identities and loyalties even more unreliable. The mixed messages of dueling mottoes transmitted throughout the war praised the power of solidarity (order) on one hand, while warning of the impending air raids and potential treachery (disorder) on the other. Britain's status vis-à-vis the rest of its dominions around the world was more unstable than ever before. One of the signs of this instability was the almost total collapse of the independent British studio system in the wake of the war. Largely taken over by Hollywood studios (which themselves suffered a few crippling blows in the early 1950s), the British system would soon be subsumed into another Anglo-American corporate model that seriously compromised the indigenous nature of British films for years to come. The myth of an authentic indigenous British national cinema is noted by transnational film

---

6. Wapshott, *Carol Reed*, xiii.

studies scholars such as Andrew Higson as being "complex, hybrid, and in flux."[7] Reed would later wander the proverbial desert searching for work directing major feature films, not unlike the lifelong exilic Orson Welles. It was only due to tremendous opportunism, professional development, and great negotiating skill that Hitchcock weathered these difficult years. Reed's successes were unquestioned, directing perhaps the most accomplished (and Wellesian) British film of all time, *The Third Man* (1949), and the lauded *Oliver!* (1968), which won him his second Academy Award. His failures were either notorious, like the disastrous production of *Mutiny on the Bounty* (1962), or entirely forgettable, like his final film, *The Public Eye* (1972), which all but evaporated.

A few of his midcentury films demonstrate the interest in time and timekeeping in relation to a cosmic order previously discussed in *Shadow of a Doubt* and *The Stranger*. Carol Reed's *The Stars Look Down* (1940) portrays the struggles of a British mining town. The issue of time haunts the miners as they pass by a fellow citizen bearing the sign "End of the World" who perpetually prophesies about the imminent apocalypse. The apocalypse eventually comes for six miners trapped in a cave-in for a week. The youngest trapped miner continues to question what day of the week it is, which reminds us about the significance of seeing time, or in this case, not seeing time. Modern civilization, especially in an industry so intrinsic to every other modern industry (a point the protagonist accentuates in a speech given in favor of the worker's rights), is based on the mechanistic regulation of time by clocks and calendars. The Judeo-Christian liturgical seven-day week is likewise based on regulating time. When the eldest miners realize that they will soon die, they begin to read from the Bible, which prompts the youngest to wonder why they are praying. "It isn't Sunday, is it?"[8] he asks, just beginning to realize his own mortality. In the case of the trapped workers whose lights begin to fail, the inability to see time emphasizes how poignant this experience of time is on an existential level.

A Kid for Two Farthings, a film Reed directed in 1953, dramatizes the effect a boy's imagination ostensibly has on his working-class London neighbors. Believing his one-horned goat to be a wish-granting unicorn, the boy wishes for good things to happen to these people at crucial moments, such as helping a wrestler win his bout, a girl marry her boyfriend, and a tailor acquire a new machine. The film's establishing and concluding shots both show Saint Paul's Cathedral in central London, framing the entire film in between perhaps the most prominent icon of the ideological

---

7. Higson, "Great Britain," 245.
8. Reed, *Stars Look Down*, 1:28:34.

state apparatus, a national building for worship famously known around the postwar world for surviving the Blitz. The opening scene clearly shows the facade of Saint Paul's clock tower, which further associates chronometry with the conflation of religion and state. The playful exploration of the possibilities of volition (i.e., wishing or praying) on the course of historical events points out the contingency of time, suggesting that chronology may or may not be tied directly to human agency. Where *The Stars Look Down* illustrates the meaning of looking at time on a human existential level, *A Kid for Two Farthings* illustrates the meaning of looking at time from a perspective of transcendence. Both demonstrate the problems of self-delusion and wish-fulfillment in a milieu permeated by mechanistic time.

Reed's 1948 Graham Greene collaboration, *The Fallen Idol*, also uses the iconography of chronometry to great effect. Set in an embassy, the butler is accused of killing his wife, and the last half an hour of the film is set *in situ* during the police investigation. While interrogating the butler in private, the chief detective orders his subordinate to give his chiming pocket watch to the boy in the butler's charge in order to keep him out of trouble. The gift of watching time is thereby offered by the authorities representing law and order. While interrogating another embassy worker about her illicit and potentially incriminating relationship with the butler, another emblem of watching time is introduced. In the middle of their questioning, a horologist invades the room and works on the prominent table clock. The suspense is created by the caesura in questions, mainly dealing with units of time and duration. "And all the time," the detective asks, "you were carrying on an affair?"[9] The answer is not given due to the intruder, who informs them that his work cannot be rushed. The interrogation scene is tightly packed with details about watching the time. The clock winder states, "Won't be a moment" and "We behave much better if [the clocks] are looked after."[10] After he mechanistically recalibrates the clock, he leaves. The interrogation begins again, continuing to insinuate the state's authority in a space protected by diplomatic immunity. The suspense of temporality is thus invoked by clocks and watches by a film that is essentially an inquiry into issues of justice. "Carol Reed deliberately added this clock winder scene to Greene's story."[11] Michael Powell fittingly said that Carol Reed "could put a film together like a watchmaker puts together a watch."[12]

---

9. Reed, *Fallen Idol*, 1:24:20–1:24:24.
10. Reed, *Fallen Idol*, 1:24:36, 1:24:50–1:24:55.
11. Wapshott, "Enchanted Moment," 21.
12. Thomson, "Reeds and Trees," 14.

Perhaps the most famous of all films directed by Carol Reed is the suspense classic *The Third Man* (1949). So much has already been discussed relating the film to the work of Orson Welles and Alfred Hitchcock that it is hardly worthwhile to revisit these points, except for the singular point that the modern cosmological presumption is manifested in some midcentury suspense films that shared their personnel and their zeitgeist. The fact that *Citizen Kane* was well known even in wartime Britain and that Reed purposefully cast Mercury Theater regular and antagonist of *Shadow of a Doubt* Joseph Cotten as the lead and Orson Welles as his estranged villain friend highlights such interconnections between the various films and worldviews at the time. As in his other films, *The Third Man* illustrates a concern with the relevance of time in a modern context. Set in the backwash of Vienna during the immediate postwar period, the film focuses on the violent convergence of the medieval and the modern, a contraction rendered cinematic in the juxtaposition of modern buildings filmed as Gothic ruins.

The film is haunted by the proverbial ghost of Harry Lime, a notorious racketeer who faked his own death to escape justice. The conclusion of Harry's and the protagonist's reunion is punctuated by perhaps the most famous speech of the film, one that Welles himself added to the script. Trying to cheer up his friend, the charismatic Lime says, "In Italy for 30 years under the Borgias they had warfare, terror, murder, and bloodshed, but they produced Michelangelo, Leonardo da Vinci, and the Renaissance. In Switzerland they had brotherly love, they had 500 years of democracy and peace, and what did that produce? The cuckoo clock."[13] The geohistorical link between ideology and cultural production, so wittily conjured by this passage, once again orients a midcentury suspense film in relation to watching cosmic time.

In the "Introduction" to the Criterion DVD of *The Third Man*, Peter Bogdanovich, perhaps the most famous American filmmaker/writer supporting the auteurist position, said, "I think *The Third Man* is one of the best, if not the greatest, nonauteur film ever made."[14] He first acknowledges the contributions of writer Graham Greene and producer Alexander Korda before discussing some of director Carol Reed's contributions to the film. He notes that Reed was a very skilled director and highly regarded before his death and implies that being considered a nonauteur is not derogatory.

Carol Reed's own stated approach to directing films resonates with this theme throughout his films. By the 1940s, he expressed an interest in films whose endings are not determined by the conventions of their genre.

---

13. Welles and Bogdanovich, *This Is Orson Welles*, 221.

14. Bogdanovich, "Introduction," 0:00:10–0:00:20.

"In time," he said, "I believe we shall get away from the eternal happy ending. It is difficult to get an audience really interested in the problems of two main characters of a story when they know in the end it will work out all right, however difficult it may seem."[15] For example, although *The Stars Look Down* contains some passing elements of romantic comedy in the middle section (which were imposed on Reed), the film's ending has an air of unpredictability about it, a lesson learned by all masters of filmed suspense. In other words, film as a microcosm of transcendent order is time-based and finite. The suspense will end by the conclusion of the film; what happens in the meantime may seem chaotic, but ultimately order is affirmed by the very structure of cinematic resolution. This seems particularly true of the midcentury cosmological presumption as well. For Reed, it was possible to accomplish many things with his subsequent films, but as they were still commercial products these films remained inextricably tethered to cultural and cinematic conventions. This very collective and communal fact allows us a unique insight into this particular zeitgeist.

ODD MAN IN

The future remained uncertain, but Reed knew he wanted to continue to direct films. Producer Alexander Korda reenergized the British film industry with his penchant for inspiring uniquely British films to be marketed worldwide, and particularly in America. He would go on to establish a unique market for these postwar films, which for a time did indeed help create a type of national cinema. It was not without limits or identity issues, but nevertheless, Korda and fellow producer Arthur Rank helped produce a kind of recognizably British film tradition that emerged from numerous years of dependence on other markets and conventions, namely those from America. For his part, Korda became the first filmmaker to be knighted by the British Crown. In 1953, Carol Reed was to become the second. One can hardly be more "establishment" than this in Great Britain. In the 1940s, Reed shared Korda's enthusiasm, explaining that British films ought to retain their unique character rather than Americanizing dialogue, accents, settings, and casting that may be unfamiliar to American audiences. "A good picture is a good picture," he said. Audiences will still be drawn to a quality film regardless of the cultural barriers. "That's still the only box-office test."[16] From a production standpoint, this was and remains a gamble predicated

---

15. Wapshott, *Carol Reed*, 114.
16. Wapshott, *Carol Reed*, 173.

on the belief that American audiences may explore cultural artifacts not accounted for in their parochial worldview. Ample promotion is helpful too.

In 1945, Reed was a free agent, looking for the next film project to follow up on the success of *The True Glory*. Within days of being published, Reed read a copy of F. L. Green's new novel, *Odd Man Out*. Published in April 1945, the book takes place entirely in contemporary Northern Ireland and portrays the struggle of a compromised IRA-like heist. Ostensibly political (since any portrayal of an insurgency is intrinsically political), the novel manages to elaborate on profound philosophical and religious themes, a point made clear by the author himself. The capacity of the book to almost overemphasize its apolitical nature is evidenced by its obfuscation of political terminology and its tendency to digress into internal monologue or theological dialogue. South England-born Green had moved to Belfast over ten years before and had previously written novels that focused on societal rather than political problems. The introduction to the 1982 edition reflects that the author would "be impatient of the current notion that northeast Ulster is destroying itself in its search for a political and cultural identity. He was more concerned with the notion of the individual outsider in conflict with society" than with political statements.[17] In this sense, *Odd Man Out* echoes other modern existential novels such as Albert Camus's *The Stranger* and Franz Kafka's *The Trial*, the second of which Orson Welles adapted and directed in a 1962 film of the same name. The themes of alienation and religion lift the narrative out of the particular time and location of a parochial struggle concerning political hegemony and transform them into universal meditations on the human condition during the midcentury period.

Even though Reed was in the process of finishing *The True Glory* during the final months of the war, he quickly became interested in adopting *Odd Man Out* as his next film. There had really been only one or two prominent films that had previously focused on the Irish political struggles in Ireland before this time: John Ford's early masterpiece, *The Informer* (1935), and the less-accomplished *Beloved Enemy* (1937), although neither of them could be considered British, since they were made by RKO and Samuel Goldwyn, respectively. Frank Launder's *I See a Dark Stranger* was released later in 1946 and wedded the threat of Nazi infiltration (dramatized in Orson Welles's *The Stranger*) with the threat of IRA infiltration by portraying the plot of a female IRA spy who attempts to help the Nazis during WWII.[18] The British industry so highly regulated the representation of this controversial organization that essentially no films portraying the

---

17. Green, *Odd Man Out*, vi.
18. Babington, *Launder and Gilliat*.

specific political situation in Ireland were produced during this period—another notable scotomaphilia.

But *Odd Man Out* was unlike these films. The apolitical nature of the story appealed to Reed's own reticence to politicize his films. Since propaganda is by definition message-based, it cannot fully accommodate the ambiguity required by the cinematic, or any, art form. Even his most overtly war-related films, *The Way Ahead* (1944) and *The Key* (1958), undermine any official pro-war doctrine by focusing on other more ambiguous issues such as interpersonal loyalty and duty. Reed was already familiar with Green's work, since his wife had appeared in a film adaptation of one of his earlier novels, *On the Night of the Fire* (1939). Reed chose Green himself to adapt his novel into a screenplay, a process that secured the close collaboration between the two. The film would become one of the two or three internationally recognized masterpieces in Reed's oeuvre, and certainly one of the great artistic works to deal with postwar transience. But after the European war ended on May 7, 1945, the future was still highly uncertain.

The world, as it is geopolitically constituted, was chaotic. Borders on every continent were contested, changed, or unknown. All territories formerly occupied by the Japanese empire were suddenly in flux. The Soviet Union had seized several territories. The United States military took over many others. The multinational occupation of Vienna in *The Third Man* highlights the uncertainty of the Soviet presence in Eastern Europe. Eastern China, Korea, Indochina, Indonesia, Philippines, and numerous islands in the Pacific shifted their political status. All territories formerly occupied by the German Reich were in transition as well. Germany itself was divided into two sovereign nations with two capitals. In Reed's 1953 film, *The Man Between*, the border between East and West Berlin ultimately demarcates the line between the protagonist's life and death. Poland, Czechoslovakia, Yugoslavia, Hungary, Austria, Greece, Turkey, Netherlands, France, Italy, and the Italian colonies were all in the process of changing their contested borders. North African territories, occupied Middle Eastern nations, and central Asia also experienced shifts in border perception and status, perhaps most controversially that of the formation of an Israeli state. The Indian subcontinent experienced epochal changes in its border recognition. The independence of India and its concomitant subdivision into the smaller sovereign states of Pakistan, East Pakistan (later Bangladesh), and India demonstrated the malleable nature of political borders. While the interstate system was ascendant, the independent states that constituted it demonstrated the contingent (and even imaginary) nature of state sovereignty and legitimacy, an observation that presumably encouraged numerous subsequent conflicts by insurgent, nationalist, or anti-systemic forces during the next few postcolonial decades. As is always the case in border negotiations, a small cadre of statesmen decides the fate of the geopolitically constituted world. The midcentury period was unusual in that so many of the world's states had a ubiquitous, albeit temporary, effect on the perception of sovereignty, authority, and legitimacy.

The immediate postwar period also saw the rise of unprecedented numbers of displaced people. As many as thirty million Chinese had fled the Japanese military advances and still others were displaced by the Communist insurgency. On the Indian subcontinent, partition and independence had left approximately twelve million people abandoning their homes. In Europe, millions of surviving émigrés, refugees, and exiles had moved away from their homes, some to return and some to move on. POWs, Holocaust survivors, and children repatriated during the *Kindertransport* slowly began to reorient themselves geographically. The transnational problems plaguing members of these mass displacements were exacerbated by the changing borders and new political barriers. In the late 1940s, transience became a new norm, the world itself a global diaspora.

As the world's borders and populations shifted with unique anxieties and frictions, Carol Reed did what he did best. *Odd Man Out* reflected the concerns of this dichotomous world fluctuating between domestic stability and deterioration of all sorts. Like *Shadow of a Doubt* and *The Stranger*, it would offer a rich microcosm of the cosmological presumption through its extensive use of emblems of cosmic time. The film project was picked up by British cinema impresario Arthur Rank's Two Cities production company, whose logo, the Tower Bridge in London and the chiming of Big Ben, preface the film. Interestingly, a clock also figures prominently in the final shot of Reed's *Our Man in Havana* (1959), the clock tower of Parliament. The final audio-visual symbol of that film represents the most recognizable institution of chronometry in the world, a symbol that immediately evokes the polyvalence of a victorious Allied state bearing an official ecclesiasticism. It is not simply any clock but an evocative and identifiable national/religious clock.

Odd Man Out's production personnel consisted of studio regulars. Perhaps due to personal loyalty to Reed or to the renewed *esprit de corps* of the British film industry (and the convalescing British nation), over two dozen worked with Reed on other films. A significant fourteen of the *Odd Man Out* personnel had just worked with Reed on either of his two previous projects, the war films *The Way Ahead* or *The True Glory*. Personnel who worked on *Odd Man Out* would work with Reed on over half of the total films he directed during his career. It would seem that the military-industrial catalyst somehow positively affected this confluence of technical skills. They had worked in favor of the war effort. Now they would work on a film that would highlight the need for peace. "A film made at the end of the Second World War," film scholar Peter Evans writes, "*Odd Man Out* is also a statement about a nation's surfeit of killing, not only in Ireland, but also in continental Europe, and other theatres of war."[19]

Here I would like to briefly accentuate the "nonauteur" status of the film, especially as this represents a break from traditional approaches. The remarkable continuity of personal relationships and skills must have provided some measure of security in such uncertain times for all involved. Interestingly, eight of *Odd Man Out*'s personnel also worked with Alfred Hitchcock (several on a film Hitchcock both directed and produced the following year for his newly created Transatlantic production company, *Under Capricorn*, which was shot partially in England). Cinematographer Robert Krasker, whose recent camera work on David Lean's *Brief Encounter* (1945) garnered him some attention, was brought on board. An Australian born to Austrian and French parents, Krasker had studied in Germany from the expressionists, many of whom emigrated in 1933 or soon after. He would go on to collaborate with Reed again, filming *The Third Man*, which earned him an Academy Award in 1949.

Like Robert Krasker's multinational background, the film's casting reflected the ambivalent attitude towards national identity. Although the film superficially portrays the violence of Northern Ireland, the actors offer a panoply of cosmopolitan affectations, especially accents. Several of the ensemble were cast directly from the famous Abbey theater in Dublin, which of course is the capital of the Republic of Ireland. Northern Ireland traditionally sports different regional dialects, isoglosses, and accents. One of the founding members of the theater, W. G. Fay was cast as Father Tom, the central religious figure of the film. F. J. McCormick portrays the unscrupulous Shell. McCormick had previously performed in over 500 different plays at the Abbey, creating the role of Joxer in O'Casey's *Juno and the Paycock* in 1924, which was filmed by Hitchcock in 1930. Kathleen Ryan, a newcomer, was cast for the role of Kathleen, Johnny's devotee. Ryan's parents were Republican activists in the Irish War of Independence and she had performed in a few plays in her home of Ireland. Cyril Cusack, who was born in South Africa but eventually emigrated to Ireland, had recently distinguished himself in a revival of J. M. Synge's *The Playboy of the Western World*. Denis O'Dea's heavy Southern Irish accent further offers a complex assortment of national and linguistic compositions. Curiously, O'Dea was cast as the Royal Ulster Constabulary chief detective, the main agent of British authority in Belfast. The range of varied or Southern Irish accents, in a film ostensibly *about* Northern Ireland, helps produce an array of hybrid cultural affectations and identities.

---

19. Evans, *Carol Reed*, 71.

Broadening this hybridity is the casting of James Mason in the title role. Perhaps the most thoroughly British up-and-coming actor at the time, Mason portrays Johnny McQueen, the leader of a burglary attempt to raise funds for the "organization." His performance in the popular and Academy Award-winning melodrama *The Seventh Veil* earlier in the year established his credibility among producers, directors, critics, and audiences alike. His half-whispering voice barely covers his characteristic British inflection. Since Johnny is supposed to be a thorough-going Irish patriot and ideologue, Mason's casting is significant. The overall effect of these diversely semi-Irish performances, with their sometimes-subtle nuances in accent, is one of ambiguous identity. The idiosyncratic casting is one of the elements that exhibits what John Hill terms the film's "decontextualising logic," a logic that has some cinematic support and may constitute a subtle critique of the sanctity of political identity.[20] Reed's own view suggests ambiguous feelings concerning the issue. With less concern for the film as a political manifesto than as a meditation on transcendent themes, Reed displayed his understated savvy for anticipating what audiences were and were not willing to accept.

The leitmotif of hybridity in the film contrasts with one's expectation of political proselytizing. Perhaps this is understandable considering that, from a strictly managerial standpoint, the film was a British production. Although permission was granted to film on location in Belfast by many key government officials in Northern Ireland, the location shooting was abbreviated and relocated to areas in and around London, truly earning the stamp of a Two Cities production. The Anglo-Irish shooting of the film production adds to the overall transnational nature of the film. Downplaying the politics (which both the novel and the film seem to do) was integral to making the story palatable, especially for British producers, officials, and audiences alike. The film premiered in London on January 30, 1947, to great success, and when it premiered in Belfast a few weeks later it drew the largest crowds in nearly twenty years.[21] The next year it won a BAFTA for the Best British Film and received an Academy Award nomination for Best Editing, putatively showing the establishment's endorsement of this worldview. Both popular and commercial, the film seemed to connect with the zeitgeist of a world that had just begun to transform from wartime chaos to postwar order. As scholars of the film have shown, the film has since become a reference point for filmic representation of the troubles of partition, further extending its influence across time and space.

---

20. Hill, *Cinema and Northern Ireland*, 126.
21. Hill, *Cinema and Northern Ireland*, 125.

DISORDERLY CONDUCT

With literally dozens of specific audio and visual references to timekeeping devices, *Odd Man Out*, as James DeFelice observes, is "a film filled with clocks."[22] As previous evidence suggests, a film filled with clocks is also a film concerned with mechanistic time and the cosmological presumption in the modern world. Like *Shadow of a Doubt* and *The Stranger*, *Odd Man Out* also illustrates the various interconnections with the cosmological worldview and geopolitical events in the midcentury period. There are two sides of the same coin to be discussed here: order and disorder. To understand the *Weltanschauung* represented in this film, we may consider the most recent geopolitical events to affect the population that produced it. During the night of April 15, 1941, approximately two hundred German Luftwaffe bombers destroyed significant sections of Belfast, killing nearly one thousand people and leaving almost hundreds of thousands homeless. In just a few short hours, the city suffered the single greatest loss of life in the entire Blitz, with the notable exception of London. Incendiary bombs and their consequent fires destroyed much of the area, and the strategic dockyards were tremendously disrupted for a significant duration.[23] At the time of the filming five years later, Belfast was still dealing with the aftermath. The loss of infrastructure and human life was devastating, but the residents began to eventually rebuild. Disorder caused by human agency was thereby countered by the orderly imperatives of others.

As dramatized in *The Third Man*, while the geopolitically constituted world strove for a reestablishment of ordered civilization, rival organizations fulfilled the socioeconomic needs of its polity. Underground movements, organized crime, black market economies, and anti-systemic insurgencies gained renewed impetus. But interestingly, the IRA, one of whose stated goals was the reclamation of Northern Ireland, found little success through its insurgency against Great Britain. A campaign begun at the beginning of WWII threatened to further destabilize Great Britain during the Axis onslaught. However, the campaign was ultimately underfunded and ineffective. It sought some tactical advantage by associating with the German Nazi Party, but little effort was put into this gambit by the Reich. The IRA offensive eventually petered out by the end of the war and of course was damned by their associations with such a nefarious enemy of the British people, an effect that alienated even British sympathizers. Neither the book nor the film explicitly identify the "organization" as the IRA, a point that is not irrelevant.

22. DeFelice, *Filmguide*, 48.
23. Douds, *Belfast Blitz*, 63.

This serves as another aspect of the film's "decontextualising logic." Why does the "organization" have to be IRA? Why not Sinn Fein or organized crime? Nonetheless, the common assumption is that the group that planned the raid on the bank at the outset of the film is indeed the IRA; yet, in reality, it could have been any one of dozens of underground groups from around the world.

By the same token, the British Royal Ulster Constabulary also suffered by being associated with the Nazis. In his epistolary objection to the filmmakers' request for permission to film in Belfast, the actual head of the RUC, Richard Pim, suggested it unwise "to provide armoured or cage cars for which the Company has asked." He went on to explain that this might be "looked upon as evidence of Gestapo methods" by the police.[24] The ultimate victory of law and order at the film's conclusion would have been unexceptional in a Hollywood film due to censorship by the Hays and Breen commissions. But in an essentially British film about Northern Ireland, as John Hill observes, "it is clearly more problematic . . . not only because of the violence involved (at a time when the police in Belfast were not themselves armed) but also the politically contested character of the police."[25] Among Allied countries, the derogatory term "Nazi" came to connote not only a certain political or ideological identity but more importantly a structure of oppression by an armed ideological police force that relies on the threat and use of violence. The fact that in the world outside the film both the IRA and RUC are identified as pseudo-Nazis highlights the paradox of power that order for some means destruction for others. This paradox between order and chaos was taken to its extremes during the midcentury period.

We may assume that circumstantially, the "organization" in *Odd Man Out* is IRA-like. Most, if not all, underground organizations operating covertly within and throughout a "legitimate" hegemonic state system create their own hierarchies. "I've got my orders,"[26] Johnny says at the outset of the film. Thus, even anti-systemic movements replicate the modern managerial proclivity for organization that Weber says serves as a ubiquitous hallmark for modernity. In this case, since Johnny McQueen has escaped prison, he has not only violated the cosmic order maintained by the state once, but a second time by transcending its carceral devices. "In prison," he says, "you have *time* to think."[27] The penitential mission of the modern prison system has been to punish but also to reform. Because he is a fugitive pursued by the agents of order, Johnny's independence, his faculties, and ultimately his

24. Hill, *Cinema and Northern Ireland*, 125.
25. Hill, *Cinema and Northern Ireland*, 192.
26. Reed, *Odd Man Out*, 0:07:57.
27. Reed, *Odd Man Out*, 0:06:47–0:06:50.

life are threatened, a theme echoed in Alberto Cavalcanti's Brit noir *They Made Me a Fugitive*, released just a few months after *Odd Man Out*. The city becomes a simulacrum of the prison he escaped. He even hallucinates that the bomb shelter he escapes to after being wounded (which initially offers him a modicum of chthonian comfort) is his prison cell. The bars ultimately reappear in the final scene because, in reality there is no escaping the carceral state, a state that has transformed its very social structures and human relationships into a hermetic architecture of incarceration.

The people who may or may not assist Johnny in his plight are mediated by this carceral logic, which itself is overlaid by the visual emblems of time. Rosie and Maude, for example, discuss how they ought to take care of him after they discover his identity as a renegade from justice. Their uncertainty over the implications that their own freewill involvement in preserving his life will cause resonates with many of the other vignettes throughout the film. After discovering Johnny, the cabbie similarly equivocates, measuring the implications. The cabbie decides to hedge his bets by instructing Johnny to tell the organization that he was helpful. But he also attempts to remove his culpability in the eyes of the law by dumping Johnny's body in a garbage heap. Fencie the barman, who quickly identifies Johnny, similarly takes the course of noninterventionism. Clocks are present in the mise-en-scène of all three vignettes. The clocks visually link the moral decisions concerning what to do with Johnny's docile body with the carceral logic that permeates this world.

Of course, Johnny's entire struggle is enacted in a mise-en-scène populated by mechanistic timekeeping devices, complete with the multifarious associations that have been previously discussed. Thus, "The clock marks the conclusion of a life brought to an abrupt and untimely end through devotion to a political cause; Johnny's death fulfills the requirements of a ritual drama that prioritises the eternal truths of morality over the time-locked beliefs of a political cause."[28] Johnny's time-locked "organization" is temporal and not eternal. He himself is organized by others. Whether politically, institutionally, or religiously, he is constituted by forces outside himself. "He belongs to the law,"[29] the constable claims, whereas Father Tom, representing the church, claims his soul belongs to God. Both the police and the priest are agents, not in the sense of philosophical freewill agency, but in the sense that they act as the very embodiments of the institutions they represent. But so are many of the other characters who wonder whether or not they should help Johnny. They too are the manifestations of diffuse networks of what Foucault termed biopower. Johnny's very life—not to mention the lives of

---

28. Evans, *Carol Reed*, 77.
29. Reed, *Odd Man Out*, 0:57:43.

the other characters in the film—is constituted by his own socialization into, and maintenance of, systems of biopower. In a true Foucauldian sense, it appears difficult, if not impossible, to ultimately escape. The film's depressed ending seems to lend an inflection to this assumption.

The film begins with a heist plan, which itself is mediated by the sounds of the Albert Memorial Clock in downtown Belfast. The plan has been carefully thought through, complete with the necessary time line. As the gang members prepare to begin their raid, the bell tolls again, after which Johnny reassures them, "There's no hurry. There's time for a cup of tea."[30] The plan is a method for organizing future time and space. It is an expectation of labor projected onto a time that has not yet occurred. The plan (as any plan intrinsically does) theorizes temporal order in relation to the fundamentally unknowable. What begins as an intrinsically suspenseful heist genre film is quickly ruptured. The plan not only goes awry in the first few minutes of the film, but the genre conventions are suddenly transformed, retaining and sustaining the fundamental element of suspense until the film's conclusion. The intensity of this cinematic rupture is declared by the violence that indicates it. In fact, the violence intensifies the suspense because we soon learn that Johnny has been wounded, perhaps fatally. In addition, he is lost by his comrades and left to wander out on his own in a liminal state between life and death. But the suspenseful overtones of this violent rupture are also magnified by the unknown status of the mill worker. Johnny seems not to know whether or not the other man was killed. This effect is drawn out for the first half of the film. The fact of the man's death is eventually revealed to the audience first, before it is revealed to Johnny, which creates dramatic irony, urging us to wonder exactly when Johnny will discover that he took another's life. The unknown fate of the mill worker introduces a doubling of suspense that heightens the effect of this rupture. The suspense of Johnny's fate lasts until the final minute of the film. As in life, we simply cannot know what the film has in store for us until its conclusion.

The violent rupture, which was used to great effect in the first half of Hitchcock's *Psycho* (1960), is perhaps even more effective in *Odd Man Out*, due to the latter film's severing of even genre expectations. Nonetheless, the gang's plan is a pyrrhic victory. The money is, in fact, stolen but becomes incidental, as in *Psycho*, an afterthought mentioned only in passing later on. But Johnny is killed, not without first suffering a Christ-like passion throughout metropolitan Belfast. The disorder that is introduced early in the film colors Johnny's journey—and is tinged with reminders of temporality. The associations between time and disorder continue when a brawl erupts in the

---

30. Reed, *Odd Man Out*, 0:03:13.

Crown Bar, necessitating Fencie to push the hands of the clock ahead to signal closing time. Even this absurd event continues to highlight the pertinent themes of the film. The fighting in the bar (although clearly unwelcomed by the establishment), seems normalized enough that by simply showing the clock at closing time it is hoped that those involved in the violence will come to their senses. The clock reminds them of the law and order that pervades their intellectually, politically, and religiously constituted world. The act of looking at time is used totemistically to stave off disorder.

The emphasis on connotative chronometry is rendered filmic by the formal cinematic elements, especially sound effects and editing. The sound editor, Harry Miller, had worked with Reed on *The Way Ahead*. But he also previously served as the editor of perhaps the most historically important British sound film, Alfred Hitchcock's *Blackmail* (1929). Miller's work on the film is notable here for a few immediate reasons. The film is considered to be the first British feature with a diegetic soundtrack. Miller started his career by dealing with the then highly unique challenges of recording and replicating sounds effectively for a film. It also continues this resonance between Hitchcock's and Reed's professional and conceptual worldviews. Miller's work on *Blackmail* and *Odd Man Out* demonstrated his innovation and attention to detail so necessary to creating an effective work of cinema.

As Karel Reisz observes, the regulated, mechanistic sounds in the mill conjure aural evocations of a clock, and "the dull unhurried beat of the mill stresses the slow passage of time while the men are trying to get the money away. By dividing time, so to speak, into a series of mechanically following units, the rhythmic beat of the mill makes the sequence intolerably long-drawn out."[31] In other words, it seems as if the mill is filled with clocklike sounds partially due to the effective use of the power of suggestion. The fact that the site of the heist is an industrial setting par excellence further connects the sound effects with mechanistic time and modernity. During the quiet of the heist, Nolan's whistle signals to the gang that it is time to go. The mill's clock is seen clearly in the background. Of course, the ubiquitous tolling of the Albert Memorial Clock perpetuates an aural continuity of mechanistic time, punctuating the narrative regularly. The diegetic presence of chronometry is therefore complicit in sustaining suspense throughout the film. Yet the filling of the soundtrack with clock tolling is utilized in a distinctly different way than in, say, *The Stranger*.

Fergus McDonnell, who also worked with Reed on *The Way Ahead*, was to receive an Academy Award nomination for his editing of *Odd Man Out*. The heavy reliance on continuity editing typifies most popular

---

31. Reisz, *Technique of Film Editing*, 266.

narrative films of the midcentury period. McDonnell's work is no exception to that convention. But a few aspects of the editing are notable. Continuity editing, which seems to suture shots together to form a cohesive point of view, grounds the viewing experience with a sense of order in and of itself. It is well established that such editing helps produce a cosmos in the act of watching a scene. The static medium shot-reverse shot matching seems to be extended to the point of tedium during the long discussion scene between Father Tom and the constable. The relatively uneventful series of continuity shots creates an overdetermined effect that tempers their discussion concerning the polyvalence of state and religion. In other words, the scene is about order, not only in content but also in form. In terms of dynamics, motion, or compositional variety, this scene is positioned in the doldrums. But in terms of constituting a sense of stability or order, it is the focal point. It hardly needs pointing out that the scene is also mediated by the visual presence of a clock, which appears in the background of so many shots.

Significantly, the scene provides a contrast to several of the more inventive sequences that are often identified by their divergence from mainstream styles of editing and composition. Scenes characterized by surrealism and expressionism therefore stand out even more against the contrastingly overdetermined continuity editing of the static church scene. In the bomb shelter, the pub, and Lukey's studio, Johnny's hallucinations of people he has previously encountered (both diegetic and pre-diegetic) are shot in superimposition, creating a surreal effect. The police officer he sees in the bomb shelter dissolves into an ostensibly "real" girl. He sees the people of Belfast superimposed in bubbles of his spilled drink at the pub and Father Tom superimposed amid paintings that swirl about him at Lukey's. These visual effects serve to undermine the sense of order, continuity, and realism that continuity attempts to create. Thus, the film struggles with itself, providing a formal device for both the aforementioned violent cinematic rupturing and the rupturing that displaced people in the postwar world invariably experienced amid the politics of partition.

MICROCOSMIC TIME AND SPACE

The time and place of the film are crucial referents to the cosmological presumption. Occurring in just one day in one city, the film projects its significance across time and space. It illustrates the microcosmic time shared by similar works such as James Joyce's *Ulysses*, which represents the cosmic significance of the universe in the duration of just one single day. The portentousness of this microcosmic time is evidenced by the film's existential appeal to timelessness and universality. The cosmic resides in the synergy between time and place.

Although Evans mistakenly claims that the film's plot "has unravelled over twelve hours," the film's plot depicts only eight hours.[32] In fact, it depicts exactly the final eight hours of Johnny's life, from 4:00 p.m. to midnight on this fateful day. It is worth noting that, in a film dominated by clocks (and all their connotations), the duration is especially important. The eight-hour working day became the standard peace-time temporal unit of labor, a fact that links Johnny's death with the mechanistic world of regulated timekeeping. Since the film is, inter alia, fundamentally about time, the discontinuity between diegetic time (eight hours) and running time (116 minutes) is heightened. The difference in modalities between the story and its cinematic representation create the time dilation so familiar in narrative films. There exist, of course, some narrative films that consciously adhere to a unity of diegetic and cinematic time, but these are rare. The time dilation effect always urges us to question what has occurred during the times in between what is represented. Why have they been elided? The effect produces at once a sense of cosmos (i.e., orderly creation) and absence (lapsis or disorder), illustrating the scotomaphilic effect discussed earlier. It is curious to note how strictly linear the film's narrative is. As Welles said of *The Stranger*, he was much fonder of the *in media res* technique of beginning the film with a previsioning of the final confrontation between Mary and Kindler in the clock tower. Such a nonchronological narrative structuring, which Welles used to great effect in *Citizen Kane*, intrinsically produces the conditions for suspense in the viewer. But in *Odd Man Out*, the linear nature of the narrative produces another kind of suspense in which nothing is certain. In this way, the film differs from its noir contemporaries that make heavy use of flashbacks, such as *Double Indemnity* (1944), *Mildred Pierce* (1945), *Sorry, Wrong Number* (1948), and *D.O.A.* (1949).

While in numerous ways the film focuses our attention on the significance of time, it also orients time within a geographic context. Although the film is clearly set in Belfast, Northern Ireland in the mid-1940s, the film attempts to decontextualize its absolute location. The fact that filming occurred in a few different places, such as the city of Belfast and Denham Film Studios in London (the film site of *Brief Encounter* and *49th Parallel*, and later used as a renowned film recording studio by the likes of Bernard Herrmann for *Vertigo*), as well as the Shoreditch and Islington neighborhoods in London further disembodies the mise-en-scène from its presumed local specificity. Even though it may be due to budgetary or logistical restrictions,

32. Evans, *Carol Reed*, 77.

the highly artificial backdrop behind the junkyard set where Shell first encounters Johnny accentuates the tenuousness of location. The harbor scene similarly consists of rather flat-looking set pieces. Both the junkyard and the harbor are aurally linked to the outside world by a train whistle and ship's horn, respectively. As in *The Night of the Hunter* (1955), these flimsy-looking sets create an expressionistic quality that heightens the temporal nature of geographic identity.

However, these decontextualizing tactics notwithstanding, the film's disembodiment of place is ultimately incomplete and unsuccessful. We know the film is about Northern Ireland in the 1940s through an abundance of circumstantial evidence. The post-title scroll informs us of its setting. Even the cover of the novel's 1982 edition is a map, labeled prominently "Plan of Belfast." Besides the presumptions concerning the IRA and the affectations of the actors, two blatant landmarks concretize the film's setting: the Albert Memorial Clock Tower and the map used in the film. The Albert Memorial Clock Tower's façade remains a distinctive Belfast icon, although it suffered minor damage from an IRA bomb explosion in 1992. While the gang members struggle to escape the chaos they created during the heist, the film presents a short montage of RUC officers searching the city.

The montage culminates with a single shot of a map, the significance of which is accented by the crescendo and then cessation of the scoring. The map, framed with no other signifiers, appears to be a map of Belfast, displaying its twisted premodern configurations of streets and alleys. Superficially, the condensation of cartographic details highlights the labyrinthine arena that should present only great possibilities for the gang's evasion, especially since we know they have the advantages of local knowledge and careful preparation. But the film animates the map, creating two simultaneous effects.

First, the manner in which the map is presented privileges our perspective. As with most maps, this map offers a high-angle perspective of the environs, as if from the position of a great imaginary height. The bird's-eye view transcends and supersedes any knowledge acquired on the street level. It is, if you will, suspended above the earth and thus perpetuates the narrative suspense. Of course, as we have been previously shown by the montage, the officers are actively searching on the ground. So the coordination of superior knowledge provided from the map and the local knowledge provided by an assertive police force has a multiplier effect. This coordination, fundamental to all modern military campaigns, was taken to its extremes during WWII, when maps, aerial photographs, and stereophotographic projections were produced at unprecedented rates. The search for the perpetrators has become a quasi-military operation and we are recruited through this epistemological privileging to act as participant-voyeurs in another kind of war.

The shot is framed so as to be filled by the map, temporarily fusing our cinematic spectatorship with cartographic spectatorship. And then the map is animated by a single arm boldly scribing a dark, semicircular border around the city with a drawing utensil. This motion suggests that the police cordon has the renegades geographically contained, which presumes a difficult, if not impossible, escape. This inherently graphic act denotes that the very individuals who have just been identified by their violation of law and order have now been circumscribed within the purview of the authorities. Those who choose to stand outside of the law by their transgressive actions are first apprehended conceptually by the map's users before being apprehended physically by the authorities. In the process of reinscribing the gang members on a map, the anonymous arm also casts a prominent shadow over the city. It foreshadows the natural darkness that will soon fall on the day, but it also foreshadows the symbolic darkness to come. As is often the case with the semiology of shadows, the meaning of this cartographic darkness is frustratingly ambiguous.

Taken as a whole, this police-map montage provides a simple expository effect as well. It shows us what the playing field or game board looks like. It shows us where the suspense will be played out. It is fitting then that the scene transitions directly to the anarchic children who appear a few times in the film sporadically playing their own street games that replicate the greater ongoing struggles. "I'm Johnny McQueen," one child shouts, playing an improvised rough-and-tumble game of pretend that, like the film itself, serves as a microcosm of more transcendent struggles. The children have been termed "an anarchic, inchoate, corrosive substratum of the city's consciousness," further associating them with chaos.[33] While the film eschews any doctrinal or theological conflict between Catholics or Protestants, it is notable that the areas represented on the map constitute the striking demographic juxtaposition of the heaviest Catholic and Protestant areas of downtown Belfast. Considering the intentions of the filmmakers (and author), the location was probably chosen more for the variety of different worldviews in this cosmopolitan area than to comment on specific denominational contentions.

The privileged position of superior cartographic/cinematic epistemology is prefigured by the establishing shots. The racking aerial shots flying increasingly more closely into the city introduce the audience to the film's basic geography. But is also places us in the position of an attacker, not unlike that of a fighter pilot. As Paul Virilio cogently argues, such travelling

33. Vaughan, *Odd Man Out*, 22.

shots historically originated in WWI, when some combat pilots alternated firing weapons and shooting film while in flight.[34] The punning but morbid association between shooting the enemy and shooting subjects on film was already established by the 1920s. The swooping motion of the camera into the city and eventually over the dockyards recruits the audience in its penetration into the conflict. Like the combat footage of the Battle of Britain, for example, which was commonplace to contemporary audiences, *Odd Man Out* begins with a similar visual idiom, that of the target shot. The target in this establishing shot turns out to be in the very center of downtown Belfast—the Albert Memorial Clock Tower. So, having involved the spectator in a quasi-military raid, it punctuates this remarkable opening by taking aim at the most prominent public timekeeping device in Northern Ireland. Instead of hearing the shriek of a strafing attack or the whistle of a descending payload, we hear the tolling of the bell, a signal that also initiates the meeting of the gang in Kathleen's house. As if to highlight the clock even more, the film's soundtrack begins with William Alwyn's ponderous score, which temporarily coexists with the tolling bell and eventually dissolves, leaving only the sound of the bell. All this occurs while our point of view descends seemingly from the heavens to the Albert Memorial Clock Tower.

It is also important to note the axiomatic unity of time and space here. Given that the subsequent events transpire over this geographic space, it does so over the next couple hours as well. As DeFelice notes, "Reed uses the clock chimes not only symbolically to till Johnny's life away but also to establish that action is occurring simultaneously in different parts of the city."[35] When the cabbie deposits Johnny the clock is tolling 8:00. When Kathleen makes her initial escape plan with the seaman the clock is also tolling 8:00. The film thus navigates through its own time and space. The unified act of looking at both space and time reminds us of the very modern presumption that looking at anything is looking back in time. Early in the century, Einstein had already theorized what would become the foundational relationship between time, space, and vision for the age of film. The fact that light itself, one of the prerequisites of seeing anything, is subject to the gravitational pull of space provided a new scientific explanation for the phenomenon of watching a film. *Odd Man Out*, like all films, exploits the visual relationship between perception and time and space. In the case of this film, the exploitation of this relationship is manifested by the logic of verisimilitude. In other words, watching the suspense of this film set in a matrix of cinematic time and space simulates in microcosm the rational order of the universe.

34. Virilio, *War and Cinema*, 17–21.
35. DeFelice, *Filmguide*, 49.

CHRISTOLOGY/CHRONOLOGY

It is easy to reduce *Odd Man Out* to a work of religious allegory. This is due in part to the abundant and unmistakable allegorical references indicated by Christian iconography and symbolism. For example, scholar Norman Holland observes that "like Christ on the *via dolorosa*, Johnny suffers betrayal and, in the end, death."[36] Like Jesus Christ, Johnny's suffering and passion through the streets of an occupied city is colored by betrayal and death. The self-sacrificial servant-leader dying for a cause, a theme that is common in world mythology, resonates strongly with the theology of suffering embodied by Christ. Of course, it pervades popular films as well, and not only in simple narrative terms. William Alwyn's deep string legato musical leitmotif for Johnny's belabored movement resonates with many contemporary scores, such as Miklos Rozsa's evocative themes for *The Asphalt Jungle* (1950), *Julius Caesar* (1953), and *Ben-Hur* (1959). Such symbolism need not even be heavily articulated to draw the connection. However, the film readily recruits explicit visual and ideological symbols (e.g., the church) to evoke these overtones. To be sure, while not an exclusively "Western" trope, Christ's passion resonates strongly through the whole Western narrative tradition.

But the film seems to deviate from such a simple reduction. The interpretation of any allegory is fundamentally problematic, since meaning is only ever implied and only by polysemous symbols. While evoking

---

36. Holland, "Carol Reed, *Odd Man Out*," para. 4.

christological allegory, *Odd Man Out* goes beyond it as well. For example, if the film successfully constructs an allegorical narrative that parallels Johnny and Jesus, the construct itself elicits an unexpected cinematic suspense. If the final narrative of Christ's passion ends not in death but in resurrection and ascension, the film's conclusion that ostensibly ends with Johnny's death projects the fantasy of resurrection upon the post-diegetic world. Will Johnny be resurrected as Jesus was? Certainly no cinematic evidence of this exists, although the scriptural stance on this point seems clearer. If both Jesus and Johnny died for the greater cause of peace on earth, we may resurrect them by activating their principles. By offering a direct association between the two figures, the film asks us a question that fades at the end like an afterimage: What will happen to the memory of the Christlike Johnny? The final words of Reed's previous work, *The True Glory*, seem to echo here: "Now the time has come to put our victory to the test . . ."[37] Perhaps peace may indeed win out, the film has us wonder.

Interestingly, the scriptural climax of the film, Johnny's proclamation in Lukey's studio of the agape Scripture is recited out of order as it appears in the Bible. The film has already set up a context of disorder in this scene through a variety of techniques. Superimposing swirling images of artistic works onto Father Tom and blending the diegetic argument between Shell and Lukey with ambient or internal sounds in Johnny's consciousness creates a hallucinatory effect of disorientation. He suddenly rises to his feet, halting these effects. The extreme low-angle shot of Johnny frames him prominently and authoritatively in contrast to this anarchy, which establishes him as a prophet-like figure. Order emerges out of chaos, so to speak. He recites the words of Saint Paul in his first letter to the Corinthian church, a church identified at the time as cosmopolitan and morally lax. In the letter, the believers of Christ are reminded that they may accomplish many significant and worthy goals, but such are meaningless without agape. "Agape" is commonly translated from Greek to denote "love" but more appropriately denotes "charity," the kind of charity God enacted by sacrificing his son for the sake of humanity. The order in which this famous passage is recited does not correspond to the scriptural representations in any of the Bibles Johnny likely would have memorized from as a youth under Father Tom's tutelage. The Scripture is therefore not inaccurate but out of order. The disordering of the crucial passage retains the hallucinatory quality of the scene while actually undermining the sense of order that the biblical proclamation putatively achieves.

Another related element haunts this scene. The silent vision of Father Tom seems to nod in affirmation or encouragement as Johnny recites the

---

37. Reed, *True Glory*, 1:23:12–1:23:15.

biblical words of peace. Is Father Tom a memory from Johnny's past? Is he an evocation of a Father Tom he once knew now animated in a different time and place? Or is Father Tom actually communicating with Johnny supernaturally in real time? The latter possibility offers the least common interpretation. However, if Johnny has received a miraculous vision (as many saints have in Christian hagiography), it suggests that Father Tom is speaking to Johnny not from his memory but from the present as an autonomous agent. The simultaneity experienced by Johnny and Father Tom's communication transcends space. As with Charlie's mental link with her uncle in *Shadow of a Doubt*, the coincidence appears beyond unusual, pushing the experience towards a supernatural explanation. This element of spiritually transcending time is fundamental to Christian belief. Christian orthodoxy presupposes that God the Creator exists outside of time, and certain special beings can intervene in human history and transcend human history. According to doctrinal teachings, Christ's incarnation in time and space made possible the transcendence of believers beyond physical space and human time. The communion of the saints links these individuals sacramentally regardless of the temporal context of their worldly lives. Saint Clare's miracle centered on her vision of an event that ostensibly occurred hundreds of miles away at the same time.[38] It is possible that the film suggests the saintliness of Johnny by referring to this phenomenological simultaneity.

The Jesus-Johnny association with the striving for peace vis-à-vis temporal worldliness is enhanced by James Mason's cultural status in 1947. Being a conscientious objector to Britain's involvement in war during WWII could hardly have endeared him to the millions of soldiers, civilians, and statesmen who heavily implicated themselves in the violence of the war. This controversial minority opinion against "the good war," particularly when countless Allies were in the process of sacrificing their lives and livelihoods, represented a stance just a shade away from treason. Mason's own conscientious objector status perhaps mirrored the official position of neutrality adopted by the Irish Republic during the war. In fact, any Irish Republican assistance in salvaging Allied boats or providing emergency services during the Belfast Blitz threatened Ireland's neutrality throughout the war, causing the anger of both Axis and Allied powers. Ultimately, though, Mason's stardom suffered little, and, in fact, he became one of the most popular and recognizable British actors of the period. At the outset of the film, Mason's Johnny discourages the use of violence, which alerts us to his conscientious transformation, which is made especially poignant given Johnny's leadership in a quasi-military organization.

---

38. Pius XII, "Lettre Apostolique."

In fact, the practice of a self-sacrificial agape combines order with disorder. Before his imprisonment and subsequent martyrdom for confronting Nazi aggression, theologian Dietrich Bonhoeffer asserted, "When Christ calls a man, he calls him to come and die."[39] The fact that sometimes destruction can result in order (in this case, divine justice) illustrates the paradox of power once again. Kathleen's role in Johnny's demise similarly defies the allegorical framework that may be imposed on the narrative. The film ends at the docks, an *entrepôt* associated with women who sell sex, which tinges the transcendent with the illicit. Like Charlie in *Shadow of a Doubt* and Mary in *The Stranger*, Kathleen technically brings about the main character's death. One cannot claim she is an archetypical femme fatale, but she nevertheless betrays his presence to the police by shooting to alert them while she clutches Johnny to her body. Retaliating, the police fire and kill both Kathleen and Johnny, an especially violent response along the lines of John Hill's observations about the contested nature of an active, aggressive, armed state of occupation in Northern Ireland. Surely Kathleen's plan appears to have more in common with passive euthanasia, or *Liebestod*, than agape, but her deliberately nonaggressive act reiterates the pacifist overtones of his death.

The frozen angel that watches over Johnny as he lies inert in the junkyard seems to simultaneously signal the fixity of temporal human experience and the capacity for transcending that very experience. The fact that the angel is a sculpture—a literally frozen one at that—appropriates a minor theme about inertia and the pull of gravity. Human beings, especially displaced refugees or fugitives, are restricted in movement. Johnny is not only restricted by the forces of law and order and the carceral state, but by his own corporeality. His wounds almost prevent him from moving. Some of the supporting characters, including the police, further hamper his movement as well. He is quintessentially human in his very struggle with his physical limitations in the final moments of life. The angel also implies the possibility of overcoming the fundamentally mundane elements facing him as well. The angel in Christian theology and mythology is typically understood as a supernatural being, although the Hebrew word *malak* means "messenger." The only three angels named specifically in the Christian Bible are Michael, Gabriel, and Satan, and were known for their supernatural powers, mediating God's interaction with humanity. Their existence points to the divine cosmos outside the chaotic temporal world. The angel's presence therefore introduces another reference to cosmic time set in a world that replicates that order through mechanistic time associated with worldly institutions.

---

39. Bonhoeffer, *Cost of Discipleship*, 99.

Whereas in *The Stranger* the moving angel in the clock tower is suspended far above the earth, in *Odd Man Out* the frozen stationary angel is fixed to the earth.

THE ULTIMATE AUTHORITIES

Watching cosmic time figures ubiquitously in *Odd Man Out*. Numerous emblems of mechanistic time are represented by all the formal elements of the film, which are apparently synchronized throughout the city and linked to the global standards. But audio and visual references to the Albert memorial clock recur, almost fetishistically, throughout the film. The clock and its tolling frames the film proper. It appears in the background of some long shots and in close-up, low-angle shots. It even appears from a high-angle tracking shot at the outset. Its tolling regularly coexists with the other diegetic sounds on the track. Its sounds signal the mechanistic measurement of time that influences the characters' dialogue and propels the plot. The film is welded to this clock tower, which represents what we can term "time imperium."

In 1947, the British Empire was in the process of transitioning from a politically constituted global empire to the postwar commonwealth model. While not coterminous, Great Britain's sovereignty over its empire and its status in the Commonwealth of Nations briefly coexisted at this historical moment. As decolonization commenced over the next few years, British imperial hegemony became defunct. One of the crucial instruments that built, maintained, and secured that empire was mechanistic time. Victoria's reign coincided with the consolidation and standardization of mechanistic time in the late nineteenth century, which overlaid the world with a Eurocentric spatial-temporal matrix that exists to this day. The imperial sovereignty that imbued this global mechanistic time imperium with global authority was rendered largely residual after Great Britain's status was severely compromised in the postwar geopolitical world.

Thus, at the time that the film was released, the Albert Memorial Clock Tower was in the process of becoming an artifact to this residual time imperium. When her beloved husband, Prince Albert, died in 1861, Victoria spearheaded a movement that memorialized him throughout the empire. From Lake Albert in Uganda to Royal Albert Hall in London, the British Empire subsequently stamped the world with memorial eponyms posthumously commemorating the Queen's consort.[40] The Albert Memorial Clock Tower in Belfast factored into this enterprising program. Completed in 1870,

---

40. Rappaport, *Magnificent Obsession*, 177.

the clock tower displays a sculpture of Prince Albert on the same side as the clockface and remains a working artifact of Victorian values and worldview. This singular public monument standing in downtown Belfast, then, simultaneously references Queen Victoria's *Liebestod* for her dead husband, the royal Victorian legacy in the British Empire, that empire's controversial and contentious occupation of Northern Ireland, the identification of Northern Ireland with other occupied territories around the world, and the polyvalent emblems of mechanistic time characteristic of high modernity that fostered this occupation. Watching cosmic time in *Odd Man Out* is manifested in the high profile the Albert Memorial Clock Tower is given in our experience of the film. Even Johnny's surname, McQueen, seems to refer to the Queen's royal vestigial presence in Northern Ireland.

The time imperium that is so present in the film helps to indicate the notion of ultimate authorities. In the film, it may be asked: What are the final authorities? In a highly polyvalent modernity, it is no surprise that both the church and the state retain an imbricated authority over temporal affairs. In terms of civil affairs, temporal law and order are maintained by the state through the threat and active use of violence, which relegates the spiritual (and thus eternal) issues to that of the church. The renegades are terminated. Father Tom, representing the church's authority, witnesses and survives the killing. As he walks away with Shell in the final shot, the camera drifts up and away from this religious figure to focus on the Albert Memorial Clock once again. The clock's knell signifies the finality of Johnny's life and the end of the film. But it also evokes the multifarious associations that have been previously established. Victoria's love for Albert, as memorialized by an emblem of time imperium, is echoed by the church's love for Johnny.

Father Tom's peaceful, charitable interest in Johnny's temporal and eternal salvation is stereotypical of Jesus's inclusion of marginalized people, an approach that seems to counter the common interpretation of Saint Paul's admonition in Romans 13:1 that "everyone must submit himself to the governing authorities, for there is no authority except that which God has established." Father Tom does not passively enable the constable to justify the state's treatment of Johnny, nor does he blindly comply with Shell's scheme to sell him out. He likewise confronts Kathleen when she implies that she will attempt to bring about his fate before the state apprehends him. The two components of the Augustinian duality of soul and body are relegated to two different authorities. Johnny's body, which is temporal, is apprehended by the police, acting under color of the law. Johnny's soul, which is eternal, has been prepared for its journey to the afterlife by the concern and teachings of the church, presumably by Father Tom himself. But neither the state nor the church are entirely successful in exerting their dominion over Johnny's being. The state destroyed a subject that by all rights should have been reincarcerated and tried with due process of law, which could have brought about a temporal justice that presupposes juridical orderliness. Father Tom was not able to reach Johnny in time to compel him to ask forgiveness or clear his conscience, which could have brought about a spiritual justice that presupposes divine orderliness. Ultimately, neither authority fully succeeds in reestablishing a microcosmic sense of cosmos.

But the Albert Memorial Clock Tower figures prominently in this regard as well. The mechanistic orderliness of the universe (presumed by the cosmological worldview) is suggested by seeing and hearing the ubiquitous clock. It preexists Johnny's passion (and his life) and will continue to exist afterwards. Johnny's life (not to mention our own) is oriented in between the measurements of the clock, a clock whose activity seems to go on forever. The duration of a life—any life—can be measured visually against such a chronometer only after it is finished. In order to ratify the cosmic nature of this relationship between measuring the duration of life against mechanistic time, the crucial time line for escape Kathleen has organized is oriented in relation to astronomical forces beyond her control. She has coordinated Johnny's escape by way of the sea. The seaman warns her that she must bring him to the ship first by 11:00 (and later by 12:00) or else they will encounter the tide. It is the gravitational pull of the moon on the oceans of Earth that predetermine the escape time line. If they wait too long, a disaster will occur. Associating Johnny's time of escape with the uncontrollable and astronomical forces of space and physical, heavenly bodies expands the spatial-temporal dimensions of Johnny's escape to what lies beyond in the cosmos. The lunar and terrestrial forces create the regulation of a natural time, impinged upon by cosmic forces that directly results in Johnny's death since the escape ship sails off when it is supposed to. Such an orientation is intrinsically based on watching the time—a cosmic time that transcends all political and physical borders on the planet. In relation to the temporal dominions of church and state, cosmic time represents the ultimate authority.

Conclusion: Things to Come

Clearly, we are living in radical continuity with the past. Long after the Holocaust ended, new mutations of genocide continue to emerge. Racism has found new manifestations. Fascist regimes have seized power in many democracies. Class disparities widen. Environmental devastation deepens. Borders continue to shift. Transnational populations are uprooted by war and famine. As we approach the middle of the twenty-first century, the influence of the middle of the twentieth century seems especially resonant. Despite the suspense of temporality, the very act of watching films in our milieu helps maintain this continuity. The cultural coding of watching cosmic time (as has genocide, for example) has changed, but remains in continuity with the past. Digital projection, computer-generated images, and quantum computing have changed the rhetorical situation within which we watch cosmic time. But it seems apparent that as a network of interconnected phenomena the tenacious, albeit tenuous, cosmological presumption still resides in contemporary cinema culture.

In *Simulacra and Simulation*, Jean Baudrillard writes, "In a violent and contemporary period of history (let's say between the two world wars and the cold war), it is myth that invades cinema as imaginary content. Myth, chased from the real by the violence of history, finds refuge in cinema."[1] Many combat films produced in the wake of the Vietnam War, for example, display a decidedly defeatist or micro-apocalyptic tone. Writing of Vietnam films, Owen Gilman states, "Everything is made up in motion through time and space; no pattern of meaning holds from one moment to the next. Unless, of course, one is prepared to accept the primacy of chaos itself as a system with a strange kind of meaning."[2] Gilman may have been describing the "hyper-kinetic realm" of combat experience in the Vietnam War problematized by its representation on film, but he might as well have been describing the apocalypse.

1. Baudrillard, *Simulacra and Simulation*, 43.
2. Gilman, "Vietnam, Chaos," 232.

Popular and critically acclaimed post-Vietnam films such as *The Deer Hunter* (1978), *Apocalypse Now* (1979), *Platoon* (1986), *Full Metal Jacket* (1987), *Black Hawk Down* (2001), and *The Hurt Locker* (2008) dramatize the moral ambiguity of American war culture. But by the same token, although such films may verge on cataclysmic if not nihilistic, the sacrifice of the protagonist(s) in the face of meaninglessness in a chaotic and morally ambivalent world can still be reinscribed as a measure of the heroic sacrifice so lauded by American combat films during WWII. Seen in this way, these films that are commonly framed as ostensibly anti-war can also be interpreted as championing the myth of redemptive violence, a myth popular in the era of combat simulations as entertainment. And of course, many popular millennial films such as *Saving Private Ryan* (1999) and *Zero Dark Thirty* (2013) merely replicate the tropes of the combat film of the 1940s and 1950s—along with the myth of redemptive violence—seemingly absent of irony or satire. Our myths about killing continue to imbue films with meaning and temper the contemporary presumption of an orderly cosmos.

"The need to organize time, to make sense of time" Conrad Oswalt states, "gives rise to the modern apocalypse, and cinematic drama is a natural medium for this ordering process, because the motion picture itself is nothing more than a meaningful arrangement of pictures."[3] The organizational potential to instantly exacerbate and mobilize sensations of outrage, anger, and hatred have been facilitated by films that in their very form represent a model of the cosmic order. From niche Christian pulp films to PAC-funded documentaries to social justice warrior agitprop, some twenty-first-century suspense films seek to elicit audience activism against a backdrop of apocalyptic geopolitical tensions. In this sense, suspense is mediated by our current situation in time and our capacity for inscribing ourselves into broad narratives that pose geopolitical chaos against cosmic order. It could even be said that contemporary digital media's privileging of the individual's sense of agency via customized programming, direct marketing, and other egocasting, enables these technocratic populations to more effectively engage with the *chaoskampf*.

Once again, the interpenetration between geopolitical suspense and cinematic suspense is played out dramatically in the traditions of cinema. The anxieties that permeate some post-Vietnam films can thus be seen as a type of movie trailer for a future apocalypse. Like agitprop, movie trailers since the interwar period have inculcated audiences in the process of perpetual desire for more entertainment. The way Laura Mulvey describes early cinema culture can be applied to the trailer as well: "An otherwise

---

3. Oswalt, "Hollywood and Armageddon," 62.

confident and competent relation to the world is suddenly faced by a sense of uncertainty."[4] The sense of suspense is only alleviated when the film is either dismissed or consumed later in time. Not unlike trailers in the midcentury period, contemporary trailers (whether projected on an IMAX screen or streaming on a subscription service) continue to prime audiences for their future consumption.

This relationship between audience/consumer and the orderliness of time/industry persists in the contemporary film experience. Insofar as we participate in cinema culture we are interpolated by these concerns on some level. This experience of interpolation hails us into its sometimes phantasmagoric world, overlaying fantasy and reality in new dramatic and even violent permutations. As Baudrillard observes, postmodern awareness of time has increasingly been extracted from the "historical real" and has been replaced instead by the hyper-real resemblance of time.[5] It could be said that contemporary (social) media operates similarly by offering a surreal and perverse set of trailers signaling tragedies that ostensibly both occurred and will occur, complete with reductive narratives, fetishized images, and intriguing threats of violence.

In the modern era, film has presented new complexities regarding the relationship between worldview and geopolitical violence. Scotomaphilia is ubiquitous and can, in some circumstances, help bring about deadly and devastating consequences such as war, torture, and genocide. In the way that watching film inherently implicates human agency neurologically in order to create meaning, watching film inherently implicates human agency morally in order to create meaning. The suspense of temporality can be simply expressed by the collision of the question "What happened?" with "What will happen?" But it also presupposes the question "Should it happen?"

So we come to the double vision or metachronic effect that has informed this book. Arguably, since the arrival of the digital age mainstream technocratic culture no longer solely or predominantly sees cosmic time as the hands of an analog clock. Whereas in the midcentury period watching the time was often synonymous with seeing the spatialized movement of the clock's hands, it is now common to conceptualize time in a de-territorialized (i.e., digital) form as well. Digital chronometers reside on computers, cell phones, dashboards, screens, and numerous other devices, often subsuming modes of watching in a dimension awash in digital information. If anything, the opportunities for metachronic films to operate as devices to watch cosmic time (and hence to perpetuate the myth of cosmic order)

---

4. Mulvey, *Death 24x a Second*, 33–34.
5. Baudrillard, *Simulacra and Simulation*, 44–45.

CONCLUSION: THINGS TO COME

have been complicated by the de-spatializing of contemporary cinema but certainly have not been eradicated by it. Something similar could be said of the anxious future faced by institutionalized religion awash in the ambiguities of contemporary and future technocracies. If we accept the secularization hypothesis, we may become "blinded" by "the role religion [has] played within the present."[6]

For cinema to exist at all, we must sustain our complicity in the maintaining of its complicated interconnection with the geopolitical concerns in which it is situated. It is my hope that this book, in part, helps shed light on some of the ways that we have been (and still are) complicit in cinema and in our world. For by exploring the frisson between the suspenseful questions "What happened?" and "What will happen?" we may come to understand the seductiveness of our own moral blind spots better, which may in turn enable us to better serve our world here and now—and after. It is high time we do.

---

6. Lackey, *Modernist God State*, 45.

Bibliography

Arendt, Hannah. *The Origins of Totalitarianism.* New York: Schocken, 2004.
Aulier, Dan. *Hitchcock's Notebooks: An Authorized and Illustrated Look inside the Creative Mind of Alfred Hitchcock.* New York: Avon, 1999.
Aveni, Anthony. *Empires in Time: Calendars, Clocks, and Cultures.* New York: Basic, 1989.
Babington, Bruce. *Launder and Gilliat.* New York: Palgrave, 2002.
Balibar, Etienne, and Immanuel Wallerstein. "Racism and Nationalism." In *Race, Nation, Class: Ambiguous Identities,* translated by Chris Turner, 37–67. London: Verso, 2002.
Barker, Kenneth, ed. *Reflecting God Study Bible.* Grand Rapids: Zondervan, 2000.
Baudrillard, Jean. *Simulacra and Simulation.* Translated by Sheila Faria Glaser. Ann Arbor: University of Michigan Press, 1994.
Bellah, Robert. "Civil Religion in America." *Daedelus* 96 (1967) 1–21.
Beloff, Max. "The Dangers of Prophecy." *History Today* 42 (1992) 8–10.
Benamou, Catherine L. *It's All True: Orson Welles's Pan-American Odyssey.* Oakland: University of California Press, 2007.
Berg, Chuck, and Tom Erskine. *The Encyclopedia of Orson Welles: From "The Hearts of Age" to "F for Fake."* Edited by John C. Tibbetts and James M. Welsh. New York: Checkmark, 2003.
Berthomé, Jean-Pierre, and François Thomas. *Orson Welles at Work.* London: Phaidon, 2008.
Best, Michael. "King John: Performance History." *Internet Shakespeare Editions.* https://internetshakespeare.uvic.ca/doc/Jn_StageHistory/section/Herbert%20Beerbohm%20Tree's%20production,%201899/index.html.
Bogdanovich, Peter. "Introduction by Writer-Director Peter Bogdanovich." In *The Third Man,* directed by Carol Reed, 4:00. 1949. New York: Canal+ Image, 2007. DVD.
Bonhoeffer, Dietrich. *The Cost of Discipleship.* Translated by Christopher Kaiser et al., with some revision by Irmgard Booth. New York: Macmillan, 1963.
Bordwell, David, et al. *The Classical Hollywood Cinema: Film Style and Mode of Production to 1960.* New York: Columbia University Press, 1985.
Brady, Frank. *Citizen Welles: A Biography of Orson Welles.* New York: Scribner, 1989.
Breton, Andre. *Manifestoes of Surrealism.* Translated by Richard Seaver and Helen R. Lane. Ann Arbor: University of Michigan Press, 2005.
Bucholz, Arden. *Moltke, Schlieffen, and Prussian War Planning.* Providence, RI: Berg, 1993.
Callow, Simon. *Hello Americans.* Vol. 2 of *Orson Welles.* New York: Viking, 2006.

———. *The Road to Xanadu*. Vol. 1 of *Orson Welles*. New York: Viking, 1995.
Chandler, Alfred. *The Visible Hand: The Managerial Revolution in American Business*. Cambridge, MA: Harvard University Press, 1993.
Cohan, Steve. *Masked Men: Masculinity and Movies in the Fifties*. Bloomington: Indiana University Press, 1997.
Conrad, Peter. *The Hitchcock Murders*. New York: Faber, 2000.
Corber, Robert. *In the Name of National Security: Hitchcock, Homophobia, and the Political Construction of Gender in Postwar America*. Durham, NC: Duke University Press, 1993.
Dallek, Robert. *Franklin D. Roosevelt: A Political Life*. New York: Viking, 2017.
DeFelice, James. *Filmguide to "Odd Man Out."* Bloomington: Indiana University Press, 1975.
Delgado, James. P. "Chapter Two: Operation Crossroads." *National Park Service*. https://www.nps.gov/parkhistory/online_books/swcrc/37/chap2.htm.
Doane, Mary Ann. *The Emergence of Cinematic Time: Modernity, Contingency, the Archive*. Cambridge: Harvard University Press, 2002.
Douds, Stephen. *The Belfast Blitz*. Newtownards, UK: Blackstaff, 2011.
Douglas, Lawrence. "Film as Witness at the International Military Tribunal." In *Genocide: A Reader*, edited by Jens Meierhenrich, 323–27. New York: Oxford University Press, 2014.
Ekirch, A. Roger. *At Day's Close: Night in Times Past*. New York: Norton, 2005.
Estrin, Mark W., ed. *Orson Welles Interviews*. Jackson: University Press of Mississippi, 2002.
Evans, Peter William. *Carol Reed*. New York: Manchester University Press, 2005.
Farrow, John, dir. *The Big Clock*. 1948. Los Angeles: Universal Pictures Home Entertainment, 2004. DVD.
Foucault, Michel. *Abnormal: Lectures at the College de France: 1974–1975*. Translated by Graham Burchell. New York: Picador, 2003.
Gabler, Neil. *An Empire of Their Own: How the Jews Invented Hollywood*. New York: Anchor, 1988.
Galison, Peter. *Einstein's Clocks, Poincare's Maps: Empires of Time*. New York: Norton, 2004.
Gear, Matthew Asprey. *At the End of the Street in the Shadow: Orson Welles and the City*. New York: Columbia University Press, 2016.
Gilman, Owen W. "Vietnam, Chaos, and the Dark Art of Improvisation." In *Inventing Vietnam: The War in Film and Television*, edited by Michael Anderegg, 231–50. Philadelphia: Temple University Press, 2009.
Goergen, Jean-Paul. "Viktor Trivas: Filmarchitekt, Regisseur, Autor Biografie." *CineGraph: Lexikon zum deutschsprachigen Film*. http://www.cinegraph.de/lexikon/Trivas_Viktor/biografie.html.
Graebner, William. *The Age of Doubt: American Thought and Culture in the 1940s*. Prospect Heights, IL: Waveland, 1991.
Grayling, A. C. *Among the Dead: The History and Moral Legacy of the WWII Bombing of Civilians in Germany and Japan*. New York: Walker, 2006.
Green, F. L. *Odd Man Out*. Boston: Rowan Tree, 1982.
Ham, Paul. *Hiroshima Nagasaki: The Real Story of the Atomic Bombings and Their Aftermath*. New York: St. Martin's, 2011.
Hamm, Thomas. *The Quakers in America*. New York: Columbia University Press, 2003.

Harris, Mark. *Five Came Back: A Story of Hollywood and the Second World War*. New York: Penguin, 2014.
Heylin, Clinton. *Despite the System: Orson Welles versus the Hollywood Studios*. Chicago: Chicago Review Press, 2005.
Higson, Andrew. "Great Britain." In *The International Movie Industry*, edited by Gorham Kindem, 234–46. Carbondale: Southern Illinois University Press, 2000.
Hill, John. *Cinema and Northern Ireland: Film, Culture and Politics*. London: British Film Institute, 2006.
Hitchcock, Alfred, dir. *North by Northwest*. 1959. Burbank, CA: Warner Bros. Pictures, 2000. DVD.
———. *Shadow of a Doubt*. 1943. Los Angeles: Universal Pictures Home Entertainment, 2000. DVD.
Holland, Norman N. "Carol Reed, *Odd Man Out* (1947)." *A Sharper Focus*. https://www.asharperfocus.com/OddMan.html.
Krohn, Bill, et al., dirs. *It's All True*. 1942. DVD. Hollywood, CA: Paramount, 1994.
Jackson, Kenneth. *Crabgrass Frontier: The Suburbanization of America*. New York: Oxford University Press, 1985.
Jancovich, Mark. "Screen Theory." In *Approaches to Popular Film*, edited by Joanne Hollows and Mark Jancovich, 123–50. Manchester, UK: Manchester University Press, 1995.
Kazal, Russell A. *Becoming Old Stock: The Paradox of German-American Identity*. Princeton, NJ: Princeton University Press, 2004.
Kennedy, John F. *Profiles in Courage*. New York: Perennial Classics, 2000.
Keynes, John Maynard. *The Essential Keynes*. Edited by Robert Skidelsky. New York: Penguin Classics, 2016.
Kolker, Robert P. *The Extraordinary Image: Orson Welles, Alfred Hitchcock, Stanley Kubrick, and the Reimagining of Cinema*. New Brunswick, NJ: Rutgers University Press, 2017.
Koontz, Claudia. *Mothers in the Fatherland: Women, the Family, and Nazi Politics*. New York: St. Martin's, 1987.
Lacey, A. R. *Bergson*. New York: Routledge, 1989.
Lackey, Michael. *The Modernist God State*. New York: Continuum, 2012.
Leaming, Barbara. *Orson Welles: A Biography*. New York: Viking, 1985.
Leff, Leonard J. *Hitchcock and Selznick: The Rich and Strange Collaboration of Alfred Hitchcock and David O. Selznick in Hollywood*. New York: Weidenfeld & Nicholson, 1987.
Longerich, Peter. *Goebbels: A Biography*. Translated by Alan Bance et al. New York: Random House, 2015.
McCombe, John P. "'Oh, I See . . .': *The Birds* and the Culmination of Hitchcock's Hyper-Romantic Vision." *Cinema Journal* 44 (2005) 64–80.
McEwan, Paul. *The Birth of a Nation*. London: Palgrave, 2015.
McGilligan, Patrick. *Alfred Hitchcock: A Life in Darkness and Light*. New York: Regan, 2003.
McLaughlin, James. "All in the Family: Alfred Hitchcock's *Shadow of a Doubt*." In *A Hitchcock Reader*, edited by Marshall Deutelbaum and Leland Poague, 141–52. Ames: Iowa State University Press, 1986.

Megargee, Geoffrey. "War of Annihilation on the Eastern Front, 1941." In *Genocide: A Reader*, edited by Jens Meierhenrich, 219–23. New York: Oxford University Press, 2014.

Metz, Christian. *Film Language: A Semiotics of the Cinema*. Chicago: Chicago University Press, 1991.

Michie, Elise. "Unveiling Maternal Desires: Hitchcock and American Domesticity." In *Hitchcock's America*, edited by Jonathan Freedman and Richard Millington, 29–53. New York: Oxford University Press, 1999.

Moss, Robert F. *The Films of Carol Reed*. New York: Columbia University Press, 1987.

Mulvey, Laura. *Death 24x a Second: Stillness and the Moving Image*. London: Reaktion, 2006.

Naremore, James. *The Magic World of Orson Welles*. Urbana: University of Illinois Press, 2015.

Nutting, Wallace. *The Clock Book: A Description of Clocks*. Framingham, MA: Old America, 1924.

Oswalt, Conrad E., Jr. "Hollywood and Armageddon: Apocalyptic Themes in Recent Cinematic Presentation." In *Screening the Sacred: Religion, Myth, and Ideology in Popular American Film*, edited by Joel W. Martin and Conrad E. Ostwalt Jr., 55–63. Boulder, CO: Westview, 1995.

Pius XII, Pope. "Lettre Apostolique Proclamant Ste Claire Patronne Céleste de la Télévision." Vatican, February 14, 1957. https://www.vatican.va/content/pius-xii/fr/apost_letters/documents/hf_p-xii_apl_21081958_st-claire.html.

Rappaport, Helen. *A Magnificent Obsession: Victoria, Albert, and the Death That Changed the British Monarchy*. New York: St. Martin's, 2011.

Reed, Carol, dir. *The Fallen Idol*. 1948. New York: Criterion, 2006. DVD.

———. *Odd Man Out*. 1947. Chatsworth, CA: Image Entertainment, 1998. DVD.

———. *The Stars Look Down*. 1940. https://archive.org/details/TheStarsLookDown1940.

Reed, Carol, and Garson Kanin, dirs. *The True Glory*. 1945. West Conshohocken, PA: Alpha Video, 2013. DVD.

Reisz, Karel. *The Technique of Film Editing*. New York: Communication Art, 1953.

Rohmer, Eric, and Claude Chabrol. *Hitchcock: The First Forty-Four Films*. Oxford: Roundhouse, 1992.

Rosenbaum, Jonathan. "The Battle over Orson Welles." In *Discovering Orson Welles*, edited by Jonathan Rosenbaum, 236–47. Berkeley: California University Press, 2007.

Ruether, Rosemary Radford. *Christianity and the Making of the Modern Family*. Boston: Beacon, 2000.

Spoto, Donald. *The Dark Side of Genius: The Life of Alfred Hitchcock*. New York: DaCapo, 1999.

Sterritt, David. *The Films of Alfred Hitchcock*. Cambridge: Cambridge University Press, 1996.

Strack, Jochen. "One German's Response to What My Nation Did in World War II." *Friends Journal* 55 (April 2010) 20–22.

Taylor, John Russell. *Hitch: The Life and Times of Alfred Hitchcock*. New York: Berkley, 1978.

Thomson, David. "Reeds and Trees." *Film Comment*. (July/August 1994) 14–23.

Truffaut, François. *Hitchcock*. With the collaboration of Helen G. Scott. New York: Simon & Schuster, 1985.

Vaughan, Dai. *Odd Man Out*. London: BFI, 1995.
Virilio, Paul. *War and Cinema: The Logistics of Perception*. Translated by Patrick Camiller. New York: Verso, 1989.
Wapshott, Nicholas. *Carol Reed: A Biography*. New York: Knopf, 1994.
———. "An Enchanted Moment." Booklet in *The Fallen Idol*, directed by Carol Reed, 18–23. 1948. New York: Criterion, 2006. DVD.
Weber, Max. *The Protestant Work Ethic and the Spirit of Capitalism*. Translated by Talcott Parsons. New York: Scribner's, 1958.
Welles, Orson, dir. *F for Fake*. 1975. New York: Criterion, 2005. DVD.
———. *The Magnificent Ambersons*. 1942. New York: Criterion, 2018. DVD.
———. *Mr. Arkadin, a.k.a. Confidential Report*. 1955. New York: Criterion, 2006. DVD.
———. *The Stranger*. 1946. West Conshohocken, PA: Alpha Video, 2002. DVD.
Welles, Orson, and Peter Bogdanovich. *This Is Orson Welles*. Edited by Jonathan Rosenbaum. New York: Harper Collins, 1992.
Wood, Robin. *Hitchcock's Films Revisited*. New York: Columbia University Press, 1989.

Index

Abbey Theater, 95
Academy Award, 26, 28, 58, 85, 88, 95, 96, 101
Across the Pacific (1942), 59
Adam, 21, 45, 73, 74
Against the Wind (1948), 84
agape, 108, 110
agency, human, 10, 16, 33, 71, 78, 79, 97, 99, 115, 116
Albert Memorial Clock, 100, 101, 104, 106, 111–13
Alice in Wonderland (1951), 5
All the President's Men (1976), 16–17
Allied War Crimes Commission, 67
Alwyn, William, 106
American War of Independence, 62, 63
Andalusian Dog, An (1928), 53
angels, 70, 71, 110, 111
Apartment, The (1960), 13
Apocalypse Now (1979), 115
apocalypse, 3, 24, 25, 56, 73, 88, 114–15
Asphalt Jungle, The (1950), 107
Atlas, 14
atomic bomb, 4, 12, 65, 66
auteur theory, 18, 28, 30, 54, 86, 90, 95
Aventure Malgache (1944), 26
axis mundi, 14

BAFTA, 96
Bank of America, 35–37, 43
Battle of Hastings, 21
Belfast, 92, 96–98, 102–104, 109, 111
Beloved Enemy (1937), 92
Ben-Hur (1959), 107

Berlin, 58, 81, 85, 93
Best Years of Our Lives, The (1946), 28, 49
Bible, 10, 51, 73, 88, 108, 110
Big Ben, 6, 94
Big Clock, The (1948), 5, 13–17
Big Red One, The (1980), 42
biopower, 99, 100
Birds, The (1963), 20, 24–25, 33
Birth of a Nation (1915), 67
Black Hawk Down (2001), 115
Black, Justice Hugo, 67
Blackmail (1929), 101
Blithe Spirit (1945), 84
Blitz, London, 89
Bogdanovich, Peter, 54, 90
Bon Voyage (1944), 19, 20, 26
Bonhoeffer, Dietrich, 110
"Bonito the Bull," 58
Bridge on the River Kwai, The (1957), 5, 58
Brief Encounter (1945), 84, 95, 103
Brit noir, 85, 99
Britain, British, 41, 47, 52, 59, 63, 69, 84–88, 90–92, 94–98, 101, 106, 109, 111, 112

calendars, 63, 88
Call Northside 777 (1948), 16
Camus, Albert, 92
Capra, Frank, 85
Carey, Macdonald, 31
Carr, E. H., 69
Carroll, Lewis, 5
Casablanca (1943), 26

cathedrals, 54, 70, 88
Catholic, 20, 21, 27, 33–36, 51, 74, 75, 105
chaos, 3, 4, 11, 18, 25, 54, 96, 98, 104, 114, 115
chaoskampf, 3, 50, 115
Chaplin, Charlie, 4
Charlie (from *Shadow of a Doubt*), 8, 28–30, 32–40, 42–46, 48, 68, 109, 110
Charlie, Uncle, 28–30, 33–40, 42–48, 54, 74
Chiang Kai-shek, 56
China, 12, 22, 93, 94
Christian, Christianity, 2, 11, 18–21, 24, 25, 27, 29, 31–34, 46, 47, 73, 74, 76, 88, 107, 109, 110, 115
chronometry, chronometer, 6, 14, 15, 41, 63, 69, 71, 89, 94, 101, 113, 116
church, 1, 8–11, 18, 21, 31, 32, 34–37, 40, 48, 53, 61, 62, 64, 68, 74, 75, 85, 99, 102, 107, 108, 112–13
Cinderella (1950), 5
cinema, 1–4, 25, 55, 59, 87, 94, 114–117
Citizen Kane (1941), 29, 50–52, 61, 90, 103
Clare, Saint, 109
Cloak and Dagger (1946), 59
clock, 1, 3–16, 20, 22, 23, 31, 32–33 35, 38, 39, 42, 43, 54, 61–65, 68–72, 75, 77, 78, 80, 81, 83, 88–90, 94, 97, 99, 101–3, 106, 111–13, 116
Clock Book, The, 68
Clock, The (1945), 5, 8
clock tower, 6, 35, 37, 40, 43, 44, 53, 63–65, 68–72, 75, 78, 81, 89, 103, 111, 112
Cohn, Harry, 55
Communism, Communist, 12, 24, 27, 33, 59, 69, 75, 77, 94
concentration camps, 47, 66, 67, 69, 76–79
Confessions of a Nazi Spy (1939), 61

conscientious objector, 109
cosmic time, 3, 4, 7, 17, 18, 48, 53–55, 110–14, 116
cosmological presumption, 1–4, 9, 12, 13, 17–20, 31, 32, 42, 48, 50, 51, 73, 84, 85, 90, 91, 94, 97, 102, 114
cosmology, 16, 19, 21, 27, 31–32, 63, 73
Cotten, Joseph, 54, 90
crypto-Nazi (see Nazi)

D.O.A. (1949), 103
"Date with Destiny," 58
Deadline USA (1952), 16
death camps (see concentration camps)
Declaration of Independence, 21
Deer Hunter, The (1978), 115
degeneracy, 38, 81
Del Rio, Dolores, 58
democracy, 10, 11, 15, 17, 26, 50, 55–56, 67, 80, 90, 114
Dial M for Murder (1954), 20
Disney, Walt, 5–7, 17
Double Indemnity (1944), 61, 103
double vision effect, 5, 6, 9, 13, 17, 18, 42, 116
Douglas, Justice William O., 66, 67
Dracula, 45
Dunning, Decla, 58

Einstein, Albert, 4, 56, 106
Eisenhower, Dwight D., 4, 62
Eisler, Hanns, 59
Eliot, T. S., 25
Escape (1940), 26
eschatology, 23–25
Europe, 3, 14, 25, 26, 28, 35, 46, 47, 49, 58, 59, 61, 70, 84, 85, 93–95
Eve, 21, 45, 73

F for Fake (1973), 54
Fallen Idol, The (1948), 89
fascism 26, 29, 47, 56, 58, 80, 114
Ferguson, Perry, 64
Foreign Correspondent (1940), 16, 26

Frederick the Great (Frederick II, King of Prussia), 81–82
French Revolution, 63
Friendly Persuasion, The (1956), 12
Full Metal Jacket (1987), 115

Gallipoli (1981), 42
genocide, 4, 42, 46, 47, 62, 67, 83, 114, 116
Gentleman's Agreement (1947), 16
Germany, German, 26, 28, 47, 59, 61–63, 67, 69, 80, 81, 82, 84, 93, 95, 97
Germany Year Zero (1948), 84
Gestapo, 98
Gilliat, Sydney, 86
God, 10, 19, 20, 25, 32–34, 42, 48, 50, 72, 73, 76, 81, 85, 99, 108–10, 112
Goebbels, Joseph, 80, 82
Good Neighbor Policy, 56, 57
Great Chain of Being, 34
Great War, The (see World War One)
Green F. L., 92, 93
Green for Danger (1946), 84
Greene, Grahame, 89, 90
Gruen wall clock, 82
guilt, 19–21, 25, 27, 76, 79

Habrecht of Strausbourg, 69
Hayworth, Rita, 57, 58, 66
Hearts of Age, The (1934), 52
heaven, 34, 46
hell, 24, 34, 46
Hemingway, Ernest, 56
hemoclysm, 4, 49
Hermann, Bernard, 103
High Noon (1952), 5, 9–13
Hirabayashi v United States (1943), 67
Hiroshima, 4, 65–66
His Girl Friday (1940), 29
history, 11, 12, 21, 25, 33, 51, 58, 61, 63, 68–71, 73, 78, 79, 82, 83, 85, 109, 114
Hitchcock, Alfred, 4, 13, 16–20, 22–30, 33, 34, 36, 37, 40, 41, 46, 47, 51, 56, 59, 65, 68, 72, 85–88, 90, 95, 100, 101

Hitler, Adolf, 4, 26, 58, 81, 82
Hollywood, 25, 26, 55–59, 77, 78, 84, 87, 98
Holocaust, The, 46, 47, 58, 65, 94, 114
Holy Family, 34, 74
Home Guard (Great Britain), 87
homosexual, 76–78
horology, horomania, 13, 61, 65, 69, 71, 79, 89
Hour Before the Dawn, The (1944), 59
House on 92nd Street, The (1945), 7, 59
House Un-American Activities Committee, The, 60
Hunchback of Notre Dame, The (1939), 70
Hurt Locker, The (2008), 115
Huston, John, 59, 60, 85
hybridity, 88, 95, 96

I Know Where I'm Going (1945), 84
I See a Dark Stranger/ The Adventuress (1946), 59, 92
ideology, ideologue, 9, 24, 25, 35, 40, 47, 50, 59, 63, 77, 79–82, 88, 90, 96, 98, 107
imperialism, 63, 85, 111
Indians (Native Americans), 6, 62
industrialization, 38, 39, 41, 42, 62, 69, 94, 101
Informer, The (1935), 92
intempesta, 39
International Court of Justice, 66
International Military Tribunal, 66
IRA (Provisional Irish Republican Army), 92, 97, 98, 104
Irish Republic, 95, 109
It's All True (1942), 53–58
Ivanhoe, 29, 46

Japan, Japanese, 4, 56, 59, 65, 66, 93, 94
Jesus Christ, 10, 30, 35, 45, 107–9, 112
Jewish people, 46, 58, 61, 69
Joseph, 33
Joyce, James, 102
Judeo-Christian (see Christian)
Judgment at Nuremberg (1961), 78
Julius Caesar (1953), 107

Kafka, Franz, 92
Key, The (1958), 93
Keynes, John Maynard, 80
Kid for Two Farthings, A (1953), 88–89
Killers, The (1946), 60
King John (1899), 86
King Kong (1933), 86
Korda, Alexander, 90, 91
Krasker, Robert, 95

Lady from Shanghai, The (1947), 58, 78
Lang, Fritz, 26, 59, 61
lapsarian, 21, 45, 73
Last Train, The (2006), 47
late, lateness, 1, 3, 5–10, 12, 21–25, 29, 32, 37–40, 42–44, 55
Latin America, 56, 58
law and order, 9, 10, 15, 21, 22, 24, 25, 34, 36, 37, 67, 89, 98, 101, 105, 110, 112
Lawrence of Arabia (1962), 58
League of Nations, 59, 67
Lean, David, 5, 86, 95
Lifeboat (1943), 26
light, 39, 88, 106
London Times, The, 69
Long Weekend, The (1943), 49
Longest Day, The (1962), 42

MacGuffin, 13
MacLeich, Archibald, 56
Magnificent Ambersons, The (1942), 53
Malachi, 10
Manchurian Candidate, The (1963), 74
Mann, Thomas, 56
Marathon Man (1976), 62
"March of Time, The," 50, 51
marriage/ married, 5, 8, 9, 11, 29, 47, 48, 57, 61, 67, 74–76, 78
Mason, James, 96, 109
McCarthy, Senator Joseph, 57, 72
McDonnell, Fergus, 101, 102
mechanistic time, 5–8, 10, 12, 14–16, 39, 41, 42, 47, 59, 69, 70, 79, 83, 89, 97, 99, 101, 110–13
Mein Kampf, 46
Merry Widow, The, 30, 44
metachronic (see double vision effect)

"Mexican Melodrama," 58
microcosm, 1, 8, 16, 17, 35, 64, 65, 77, 91, 94, 102, 105, 106, 113
Mildred Pierce (1945), 49, 103
Miller, Harry, 101
Ministry of Fear (1944), 59
miracle, miraculous, 30, 75, 109
Moon is Down, The (1943), 57
morality, 1, 2, 10, 12, 18, 20–22, 24–29, 31–38, 42, 43, 46, 47, 66, 78, 99, 108, 115–17
Mortal Storm, The (1940), 26
McQueen, Johnny, 95–96, 98–100, 102–110, 112, 113
Mr. Arkadin/ Confidential Report (1955), 52
Mrs. Miniver (1942), 28
Mutiny on the Bounty (1962), 88
myth, mythology, 34, 50, 70, 74, 87, 107, 110, 114–16

Nagasaki, 4, 66
Naked City, The (1948), 7
nation-state, 15, 16, 18
Nazi, Nazism, 4, 14, 17, 46, 47, 58, 59, 60, 61, 66, 68–70, 72, 74–83, 92, 97, 98, 110
New York City, 7, 8, 22
Newton, Sir Isaac, 31–33
Night of the Hunter (1955), 104
Night Train to Munich (1940), 87
No Man's Land/ Hell on Earth (1931), 59
Noah, 73
Normandy invasion, 85, 87
North by Northwest (1959), 19–20, 22–24
Northern Ireland, 92, 95–98, 103, 104, 106, 110, 112
Notorious (1946), 20, 23, 59

Odd Man Out (1947), 4, 5, 17, 92–112
Oliver! (1968), 88
On the Night of the Fire (1939), 93
On the Town (1949), 5, 7–9
On the Waterfront (1954), 58
Open City (1945), 84
Oscar (see Academy Award)

orrery, 33
Othello (1952), 52
Other Side of the Wind, The (2018), 52
Our Man in Havana (1959), 94
Ox-Bow Incident, The (1943), 70

Paisan (1946), 84
Paradine Case, The (1947), 24
Passport to Pimlico (1949), 84
Paul, Saint, 33, 108, 112
Peace Prize, 59, 67
Pearl Harbor, 55
Peter Pan (1953), 5, 6
Philadelphia, 30, 45
Pinky (1949), 49
Platoon (1986), 115
polyvalence, 1, 2, 9, 11, 12, 17, 18, 32, 62, 74, 85, 94, 102, 112
Powell, Michael, 86, 89
Principia Mathematica, 32
propaganda, 18, 26, 29, 35, 47, 57, 59, 60, 63, 76, 79, 80, 85, 87, 93
Protestant, 21, 105
Psycho (1960), 33, 100
psychology, 2, 3, 12, 25, 49, 56, 77, 79, 86
psychoanalysis, 7, 15, 39, 79
Public Eye, The (1972), 88

Quaker, 9, 12

racial violence, 70
railroad, 41
Rake's Progress, The (1945), 84
Rank, Arthur, 91, 94
Rankin, Charles, 14, 60–62, 65, 67–83
Rear Window (1954), 20
Rebecca (1940), 24
Reed, Carol, 4, 17, 86–96, 101, 106, 108
relativity, 31, 32, 106
Revere, Paul, 63
Revolutionary War (see American War of Independence)
Robinson, Edward G., 61
Roosevelt, Franklin, 56, 57, 60
Rope (1948), 20, 46, 65
Rose, Saint, 33

Rozsa, Miklos, 107
RUC (British Royal Ulster Constabulary), 98, 104
Rushmore, Mount, 22
Ryan, Kathleen, 95

Sabotage (1936), 20
Saboteur (1942), 26, 59, 72
sacrament, 9, 11, 47, 48, 75, 109
Saint Paul's Cathedral, 88, 89
Saint Paul (city), 33
Salute for Three (1943), 31
salvation, 16, 20, 28, 29, 34, 42, 74, 112
San Francisco, 21, 24, 33
San Juan Bautista (mission), 21, 33
San Pietro (1945), 85
Santa Rosa, 28, 31, 33–37, 40–42, 44–48, 62, 64
Saving Private Ryan (1999), 115
Scarlet Street (1945), 61
Schindler's List (1993), 47
scotomaphilia, 2–4, 78, 93, 116
Second World War, The (see World War Two)
Secret in Their Eyes, The (2009), 62
Selznick, David O., 27
Set-Up, The (1949), 49
Seven Years War, The, 82
Seventh Veil, The (1945), 96
Shadow of a Doubt (1946), 4, 5, 8, 17–48, 54, 68, 69, 88, 90, 94, 97, 109, 110
Shoah (1980), 47
Silence of the Lambs (1991), 62
sin, 21, 29, 44, 73
Snake Pit, The (1948), 49
Sorry, Wrong Number (1948), 103
Soviet Union, 69, 93
Spiegel, Sam, 58, 60
Spiral Staircase, The (1945), 46
standardization, standards, 1, 2, 12, 16, 27, 29, 36, 39–41, 65, 66, 74, 111
Stars Look Down, The (1940), 88, 89, 91
Steinbeck, John, 57
Sting, The (1973), 30
Storm Center (1956), 33

Stranger, The (1946), 4, 5, 14, 17, 49–83, 88, 92, 94, 97, 101, 103, 110, 111
Strangers on a Train (1951), 24, 34
sundial, 13, 15
surveillance, 14, 36, 40
suspense of temporality, 6, 11, 17, 42, 50, 83, 89, 114, 116

They Made Me a Fugitive (1947), 99
Third Man, The (1949), 90, 93, 95, 97
Third Reich, The, 47, 59, 81, 82, 93, 97
time imperium, 6, 14, 17, 111, 112
time zones, 1, 41
Tiomkin, Dimitri, 13
Tomorrow is Forever (1946), 57
Topaz (1968), 27
Torn Curtain (1966), 27
Touch of Evil (1958), 58
Tower Bridge, 94
trains, 1, 5, 9, 11, 19, 22, 23, 27, 37, 40–43, 45, 47, 65, 69, 79, 104
Tree, Sir Herbert Beerbohm, 86
Trivas, Victor, 58
True Glory, The (1945), 85–87, 92, 94, 108

Under Capricorn (1949), 94
United Nations, 66

V-Day (Victory Day), 50, 58, 60, 72
Veiller, Anthony, 60
Versailles Treaty, 67, 80

Vertigo (1958), 20, 21, 33, 103
Victorian, 1, 6, 45, 112
Vietnam War, 4, 114, 115

Wake Island (1942), 31
Wallace, Edgar, 86
"War of the Worlds, The" (1938 radio broadcast), 50
watch, pocket, 5, 89
watch, wrist 14, 20–22, 32
Way Ahead, The (1944), 87, 93, 94, 101
Weber, Max, 16, 55, 98
Weimar Republic, 67, 80, 81
Welles, Orson, 4, 14, 17, 28, 29, 50–61, 66, 72, 78, 85–88, 90, 92, 103
Why We Fight (1942–1945), 60, 85
Wilder, Thornton, 27, 28, 30
Wilson, Woodrow, 67
World War One, 3, 4, 25, 67, 80, 106
World War Two, 17, 18, 47, 49, 67, 71, 82, 84–86, 92, 95, 97, 104, 109, 115
Wright, Teresa, 28
Wrong Man, The (1956), 24
WWI (see World War One)
WWII (see World War Two)

xenophobia, 62

Yeats, William Butler, 25
Young, Loretta, 61, 75

Zero Dark Thirty (2013), 115

www.ingramcontent.com/pod-product-compliance
Lightning Source LLC
Chambersburg PA
CBHW020855160426
43192CB00007B/929